Still Rambling Down Life's Road...

...*with a brain injury*

Kevin Pettit

Author's Tranquility Press
ATLANTA, GEORGIA

Copyright © 2024 by Kevin Pettit

All rights reserved. No part of this publication may be reproduced, distributed or transmitted in any form or by any means, including photocopying, recording, or other electronic or mechanical methods, without the prior written permission of the publisher, except in the case of brief quotations embodied in critical reviews and certain other noncommercial uses permitted by copyright law. For permission requests, write to the publisher, addressed "Attention: Permissions Coordinator," at the address below.

Kevin Pettit/Author's Tranquility Press
3900 N Commerce Dr.Suite 300 #1255
Atlanta, GA 30344
www.authorstranquilitypress.com

Ordering Information:
Quantity sales. Special discounts are available on quantity purchases by corporations, associations, and others. For details, contact the "Special Sales Department" at the address above.

STILL RAMBLING DOWN LIFE'S ROAD/ Kevin Pettit
Library of Congress Control Number: 2024903963
Hardback: 978-1-962859-08-0
Paperback: 978-1-962859-09-7
eBook: 978-1-962859-10-3

Table of Contents

PROLOGUE 1
INTRODUCTION 5
CHAPTER 1 7
CHAPTER 2 Why am I here? 9
CHAPTER 3 My Life As An Invalid 25
CHAPTER 4 31
CHAPTER 5 Being Mentally Disabled 33
CHAPTER 6 41
CHAPTER 7 43
CHAPTER 8 45
CHAPTER 9 God Did It 47
CHAPTER 10 What I've Learned Thus Far (PART I) 51
CHAPTER 11 55
CHAPTER 12 I Deserved It 57
CHAPTER 13 61
CHAPTER 14 Surface Realities 63
CHAPTER 15 65
CHAPTER 16 A Trip on the Dark Side 67
CHAPTER 17 75
CHAPTER 18 Acceptance= ? 77
CHAPTER 19 83
CHAPTER 20 Nothing Happens by Accident 85
CHAPTER 21 Life's a Labyrinth 89
CHAPTER 22 Life, Love, and Killing Bugs 95
CHAPTER 23 What I've Learned Thus Far (PART II) 101
CHAPTER 24 I'm a Good Person 105
CHAPTER 25 My Sermon 113
CHAPTER 26 Poorly Aimed Hatred 117
CHAPTER 27 God, Sugar, and Life 123
CHAPTER 28 What I've Learned Thus Far (PART III) 135
CHAPTER 29 The Road Goes On 141
CHAPTER 30 One Loss 149
CHAPTER 31 Metaphysics and Life's Purpose 155
APPENDIX For Survivors 163
APPENDIX For Supporters 165
VISION 167

"Still Rambling Down Life's Road... with a brain injury"

Donna,

I hope that you can enjoy reading this book and learn a lot about T.B.I. from my book.

In peace,

—Keith Pettit

PROLOGUE

June 19, 2002

This is a book about my experiences resulting from a car accident. All the incidents depicted in it actually happened. Don't worry, the names (particularly one) have been changed to protect the innocent (and the guilty).

Voicing and hence clarifying my anger and other feelings helped me realize, confront, and face up to my emotions and thoughts. I became a more whole person. This is much of why I wrote this book. I decided to publish it in hopes that this book might help those who are in a similar situation, and those who care for them.

Initially I wasn't able to write, so when I started keeping a journal I put some things down from memory. The time order of certain things was difficult for me to remember early on, after my accident, so the chronology of some things may be out of order. I haven't edited my writing in the hopes that my writing quality, style, and choice of subject matter will chronicle my recovery.

In the first several chapters, my writing style is rather fragmentary which mimics my conversational style and thought processes. Rather than edit this and make the book more readable, I have left it as I wrote it to give you a sense of what my thinking was like and the challenges that I faced. Thus, the first several chapters are fragmentary but authentic. Just hold on!

I hope this book is as helpful for you to read as it was for me to write. It is designed to give you a picture from the inside out of what it has been like for me to have a traumatic brain injury (TBI). Traumatic brain injuries occur more than 2 million times each year in the United States. There are around 275 million people in the United States, so if you know 100 people, there is a good chance that every year, two of them will suffer a brain injury of some severity.

I hope that you and those you love never are forced to face a TBI, and that you are a more careful and defensive driver as a result of reading this book. One of the good things about my accident was that it caused everyone in my extended family to drive more carefully. I hope this benefit extends to you.

The events of this book coincided with the election of Jesse ("The Body") Ventura to the governorship in Minnesota. Talk about a strange period in my life. Unlike the governorship of Mr. Ventura, this chapter in my life has no term limits. I hope that I can find a way to make this incident contribute positively to my life. And I hope that we all have been affected positively.

I want to thank people without whom this book would be impossible: my family, who gave me the will to live; the doctors, nurses and technicians at Hennepin County Hospital, Swedish and Craig hospitals, and Boulder's Mapleton Hospital who sustained my life and helped me realize my life was still worth living; and most importantly my ex-wife Karen and son Andrew, whom I love dearly.

This book is dedicated to those who made it possible: my family, doctors and nurses in various places, and friends. Although this book primarily concerns my personal and not professional life, I would like to take this opportunity to thank President Steve Lewis, Dean Sam Patterson, and my physics colleagues at Carleton College, for their encouragement, and for being so flexible in helping me return to work. I also would like to extend a special thanks to Professor John Taylor of the University of Colorado, the best mentor in the world, who helped mold my teaching. Special thanks to Alan Johnson,

Prologue

Jamie Jarvis, Jane McDonnell, Ian Barbour, and Kitsey Canaan for advice on this book. I would like to extend special thanks to my good friend Doug Kenshol.

November 12, 2023

In addition, for the publication of this edition of my book with the expanded title "***Still*** Rambling Down Life's Road… with a brain injury", I need to credit and thank my mom, Ty Bliss, for her encouragement and help editing the final product of my extended considerations about living with a brain injury. I believe the three chapters that I've added, chapters 28, 29, and 30, end on a more inspirational note for others dealing with this sort of life-altering tragedy. I certainly have found a more balanced and productive life than I was living when I completed the previous version of my survival memoir. I hope that you find these additions helpful as well!

"Still Rambling Down Life's Road... with a brain injury"

INTRODUCTION

June 18, 2002

Kevin Pettit is a remarkable individual. He was involved in an auto accident on October 27, 1998 in Northfield, Minnesota. The initial assessment of his injury at Hennepin County Medical Center in Minneapolis, Minnesota was that he had sustained a severe closed head injury. He had a Glasgow Coma Scale Score of 3. This is the lowest score you can have and still be alive.

He also had multiple other traumatic injuries. This started Mr. Pettit's journey and recovery from his closed head injury. From Hennepin County Medical Center he went to the Multi Trauma Unit at Swedish Medical Center in Englewood, Colorado. This is where I first met Mr. Pettit. The right side of his body was paralyzed. He was initially mute and his prognosis was guarded according to his physicians. The goal of returning to his job as assistant professor was an odyssey that did not even seem relevant to consider. Dr. Pettit was admitted to Craig Hospital in November of 1998 and was not discharged until February of 1999. His MRI of the brain was consistent with a severe injury.

During the course of his inpatient rehabilitation, Dr. Pettit worked on overcoming many neurobehavioral problems including impulsivity, perseveration, and diminished attention/concentration. Dr. Pettit became an on-the-job expert in reacquiring the skills that are involved in basic independence. Initially, he lacked insight into his cognitive deficits but then was confronted with the terrible discrepancy between his preinjury level of functioning and the realities of his deficits.

Dr. Pettit's struggles to improve his functioning render him a unique individual. He is perhaps the only physicist in the country who can tell you what slowed speed of processing means in clear and practical psychological terms. Dr. Pettit went on to outpatient therapy at Boulder Mapleton, and in Boulder he struggled with his own personal outward-bound journey – returning to teaching. He continues to work on maximizing all aspects of himself including the melody and tone of his singing. In this volume about his recovery, Dr. Pettit provides the unique perspective of a scientist forced to confront a multitude of psychological, community and professional challenges.

Dr. Pettit's story is a remarkable work that is still in progress. It reflects his interface with health care providers in multiple States and settings. It is a testimony to the best values present in liberal arts colleges, in that his alma mater where he teaches in Minnesota has helped to enhance his recovery. His story also reflects the great utility of the support from scientific colleagues at the University of Colorado in Boulder. Dr. Pettit's story reveals the heart of a very bright and good man, as he has worked hard to create a rich and productive future in spite of a severe closed head injury. Dr. Pettit's writing captures the personal struggles involved in his journey toward the future in very personal and clear terms. It is a testimony to the best of the human spirit.

— **James Schraa**, PsyD
Director of CNI Center for Neurobehavioral Trauma &
Neurophychologist at Craig Rehabilitation Hospital

CHAPTER 1

April 15, 1999

Ms. ---,

This letter to you serves a couple of purposes. First and foremost, it is my chance to vent my frustration and anger. Second it is a chance for you to read, understand, and learn about the horrors you can cause. I hope you read through and accept this letter for the wisdom and insight it will give you and the knowledge of the danger and horror of your own driving.

Read on…

 "Still Rambling Down Life's Road... with a brain injury"

CHAPTER 2
Why am I here?

January 17, 1999

I think I should write down my thoughts. I've never kept a diary but this would be a good time to start. I hope I can remember to write in it each day. Luckily, my aunt gave me her computer. It's a laptop and it is the only way I can write.

> I, Kevin Pettit, promise that I will write in my diary every day.
>
> *[signature]*
>
> P.S. I had to have my signature copied off from my drivers' license and put here. I can't write anymore.

My memory stretches back to later-December. The first thing I remember, is having a catheter stuck into me to help me when I needed to relieve myself. Apparently, I showed no outward sign of any pain and my nurses at Craig Rehabilitation Hospital thought it was strange. It's not like you get a couple inches of fish tank tube stuck into your penis every day. But I did, several times a day. It caused major pain.

I remember not being able to speak. I had a tracheotomy. I had a little tube stuck into my throat that allowed me to breathe. They tell me that I used to be on oxygen, especially at night. They needed to make sure I was breathing OK, and that is the most difficult time to check it. It's also a time when you're most likely to have difficulty breathing, too.

A little later, it was sometimes very hard to talk especially if my hands were busy. To talk I had to put my finger over my tracheotomy hole and block it. So, if I was doing something with my hands, I couldn't talk. Talking was really difficult.

Like, one time some friends came over to sing to me for Christmas. I was really happy to see them since it had been a long time since I'd seen them. They told me how happy they were to see me and said "Merry Christmas!"

My hands were free, so I said, "Thanks, nice to see you."

They gave me a card from their mom, who I knew. When I was opening the card they said, "Where are your wife Karen and son Andrew?"

I had to put all the stuff in my hands down and set my finger over a hole in my trache tube, blocking it.

"They're at home. It's nice of you to come but it's too late for Andrew," I said.

That kind of put a rough end to our conversation, what with them talking and me having to block my trache to talk back. Oh yeah, and my speech was really slurred. That's getting better though.

As I began to breathe with more confidence, I needed oxygen and air less. The traches they put into me were made smaller and smaller. I guess they took out my last trache sometime right after Christmas. What a nice present!

Today I was with my occupational therapist, Dave. Occupational therapy is a funny name. It's not physical therapy or speech therapy.

Chapter 2: Why am I here?

It is "everything else in life" therapy. It's working on and doing everything you'd do in "normal" life.

Dave and I were playing this fun game. It was a game of questions and answers (correct ones, hopefully.)

"Who is you wife?" asked Dave.

"That's easy, Karen." I said.

"What about your family. Who are your brothers?" queried Dave. I thought about that one.

I replied, "David... Andy, and you."

Dave chuckled to himself and was concerned because that was an indication of how serious my condition was.

"No," he said, "I'm just your therapist. Who are your brothers?"

"David, Andy, and you." I replied.

Dave didn't understand me. He thought it was a mistake, but it wasn't. Not often are people around you as much as my therapists were, and it isn't often that you meet people as nice as Dave. Dave chalked that one up to another patient confusion and didn't worry about it.

"I've got to be going. See you tomorrow," he said.

"OK." I said and I started to get ready for lunch.

"Bye-bye, Mr. On-time," Dave said as he left.

I thought about my timeliness, how I keep my watch set with the NIST coordinated universal time clock, and my doctorate in physics.

"That would be Dr. On-time," I told him.

My sister overheard me and after Dave left, I told her that I had asked everyone to call me Dr. On-time. I explained that I'm the only Dr. On-time and the only doctor who is on time. She laughed.

Now, I'm not a hundred percent sure of why I am in the hospital. Apparently it is because of something related to a car accident I was in on October 20-something. I don't even know when it happened, but I am sure of one thing. I used to live in Minnesota and I was a professor of physics at Carleton College. I'm in Denver now and I'm glad I'm here because life here is certainly better than in a hospital in Minnesota. My family and my wife's family are from Boulder near Denver. I was raised in Boulder. Yes! I'm back home (and I'm lucky enough to have such a nice place to be from)!

I felt pretty hungry. Lunches were certainly good and most importantly they were free. They were a lot better than the earlier ones that I remember. Those didn't taste good (I assume). Well... they didn't actually taste.

They were delivered to me through a feeding tube. The gastro-tube (G-tube for short) was a tube that delivered sustenance directly to my stomach. The fluid looked like ground up Eggs Sardou, was green, and probably tasteless or bad tasting. I had a hole in my stomach area (and still have a scar) into which the G-tube was inserted once. I said, "It was inserted once" because it remained in me as a kind of a permanent object connected to me. I still have a scar from it, one of nine, as I'll explain later.

After lunch I get cleaned up and ready for what is to come. I had to get ready for physical therapy. It took me a while (as everything does now) and I got into my wheelchair. I wheeled myself out of the room and toward the bridge that went over the street to the side where patients who needed lots of help lived. I, too, had lived there not long ago. I needed more help too. For example, I couldn't feed myself and needed that G-tube for a while. I couldn't go to the bathroom by myself. I wore Depends. But I'm real glad I'm over all that now.

On the way over to the other side of the street I bumped into another wheelchair-bound patient. I started taking to him. We were thinking about being wheelchair bound and were both going to therapy on the other side of the street.

Chapter 2: Why am I here?

I challenged him to a race. There was a ramp between the two buildings going over the street. We started out at the beginning of the ramp going up. We were both pushing real hard and going as fast as possible, and I was in front. We started going down the ramp and our speed picked up. We crossed the finish line, I won, and I was rejoicing!

Just then my right foot started dragging on the ground. That darn clonus problem!

Clonus is fast involuntary shaking of your leg or arm. My leg jumps around really fast when I get it in the right position. It's like when you shiver. It turns out that your brain sends out calming signals to your whole body and that part of my brain got screwed up. That's why I have this clonus problem. After learning about the cause of my clonus problem, I developed a theory. When you shiver from cold your brain stops sending these calming signals to your whole body for an instant. And... my theory was right!

When I was racing across the bridge, it wasn't so easy for me to pick my right leg up because my right side is my side on which my clavicle was broken in two places, my clonus problem is worst, and I have limited range of motion. (My right side is why I was sentenced for a while to what is called the "Easy Stretcher." I prefer to call it the "Pain in the Ass Stretcher.") Anyway, after I had won the race in my wheelchair, my right leg was dragging, which caused me to run into the concrete pole on the right side.

A nurse saw this, yelled at us to stop, and was really worried.

"Are you OK?" the nurse asked after she made sure that the other patient was OK.

"Fine," I said, thankful that I hadn't really been hurt.

"Well, don't do that again," she told me.

I felt really bad about my behavior and myself, but at least I had won. Yea, I won!

The other day, I couldn't remember whom I wrestled in high school when I was a student here in Colorado. I knew his name was Gates, but I wasn't sure whom. I had to ask my brother Dave (who wrestled with me in high school) if it was Bill Gates. I was imagining that I wrestled the richest guy in America (if not the world)! I think I beat him once but lost to him in state. Yeah! I beat the richest man in the world!

But Dave had to bring me back into reality. It wasn't Bill Gates that I wrestled, but Joe Gates. Maybe they're really distant relatives.

February 2, 1999

I was thinking about work today. It turns out I must have been an OK professor because it's not at all easy to get a job at a place like Carleton. I can remember that I taught Atomic and Nuclear Physics but what else? Hmm... I can't remember.

Karen told me that last summer I submitted a grant application to a big national corporation and was awarded a grant! I have no memory of this and I hope that my memory comes back because I need to figure out what I said I'd do in my grant application.

Someone at the corporation where I submitted the grant had contacted my department's head and told them about the grant I had won. Apparently, my department was really happy and had even bought me some cake or cupcakes. That was a Monday, I think. But as it turns out my accident happened on Tuesday.

As it turns out, we were in a car accident. A pretty bad one. I don't remember everything I've learned, but I think someone ran into us on the highway. It turns out we were run into by a bad driver and it was mostly her fault. Also, I wasn't driving, Karen was. Not that I think Karen is at fault at all. She's a great driver. I'm sure it was entirely the other woman's fault.

Karen says the person that ran into us is a real shitty driver. She has had two drunken driving arrests before she hit us! Each time her license was suspended for three months. It hadn't been legal for her

Chapter 2: Why am I here?

to drive for more than two months before she hit us! I wonder if she was drunk when she hit us.

Since Karen and I were both in the hospital that night, her sister had to fly out from Washington DC to take care of Andrew. Apparently, that night (about twelve hours after the accident) this woman called our house to apologize for causing the accident! I still had about two hundred and fifty hours of coma to go! Apparently, Karen's sister hung up on her. It makes me mad to think that all she did was call to say "Sorry". How about being more careful when you're driving and not speeding.

But, to get back to what I was saying...

So my department was going to give me the cake or cupcakes on Tuesday or Wednesday for my award. I never showed up, obviously. They must have thrown the cakes away or they must have hated eating them. I have such a great department. I'm really looking forward to when I can teach again.

I'm looking forward to when I can leave Craig and start my job again. I used to think that I should leave Craig by Dec. 20. I felt very lucky to be at Craig – I thought that I didn't deserve to be taking up such space when there are people who *really* need it.

I guess that was I having a hard time understanding the magnitude of a TBI. People tell me that it doesn't heal in a couple of months. It takes a lot longer. The other day I was told that it takes a minimum of two to five years to heal (if you ever heal). I wish I had lost a leg or something like that. It would have been a lot easier.

The other night my family and I went to a movie. My brother, David, suggested that we go see a new *Star Trek* movie called *Insurrection*. I was excited because I watch *Star Trek* a lot. Basically I have it on from four o'clock until bedtime every night. I am Mr. Star Trek Dr. Star Trek and have people call me that way.

"All right, a new *Star Trek* movie," I thought and got ready to go. I'd be going with my two brothers, my brother-in-law, and Karen. We went to the movie and I loved it.

At one point the captain says to the first officer,

"Time is a companion who goes with us on the journey and reminds us to cherish every moment ... because they'll never come again. What we leave behind is not as important as how we've lived."

That line affected me tons. Very quickly, I wrote it down on a paper notepad that I always keep with me so that I can record things that I'd like to remember. The line expresses the drastic importance of the life you live and living life to the fullest. You don't realize how important life is until you've come so close to losing it. I think I have experienced something really tough: having a view on both sides of the death sheet.

Dying is one thing: it's actually not that tough. The other night I had some pretty depressing thoughts. I was considering suicide by shooting myself in the head. I was thinking about all the strain I must have been causing everyone in my family.

It's one thing having a two-and-a-half-year-old son like Andrew. It's totally different with a husband who needs much more assistance than your son. Sure, my death would be sad. It would probably take my wife Karen a year (maybe two) to get over. But then she could find someone else, marry him, and be happy with him. End of story. But with me, I figured, life would be this bad forever.

But sitting here in the hospital and looking outside at the beautiful weather, I'm finding that life is such a good thing. I wish I could show everyone how great life is even in the worst moments. I was thinking of having a sort of dirge or wake next October on the anniversary of our crash. But now I think it would be a great time to throw a party to celebrate life! Not many people have seen death as I have and come back to tell about it.

Chapter 2: Why am I here?

It must be that I like watching *Star Trek* so much because I can remember it OK. I've been told that a TBI affects your short-term memory most and that usually your long term isn't as badly affected. If I knew a movie pretty well before my accident, then I could enjoy it more easily after my accident because, at the end of the movie, I could remember what happened at the beginning of it. It's just very hard for me to watch a new movie and enjoy it because I forget the plot as it is developing.

September 2, 2002

Yesterday, I was cleaning out a desk in my study and I found a journal that was kept by my family when I was housed in the hospitals in Denver starting about 1 month after my injury. I thought that maybe I should include some excerpts of it so that the reader would get a sense of where I was in the early stage of my recovery.

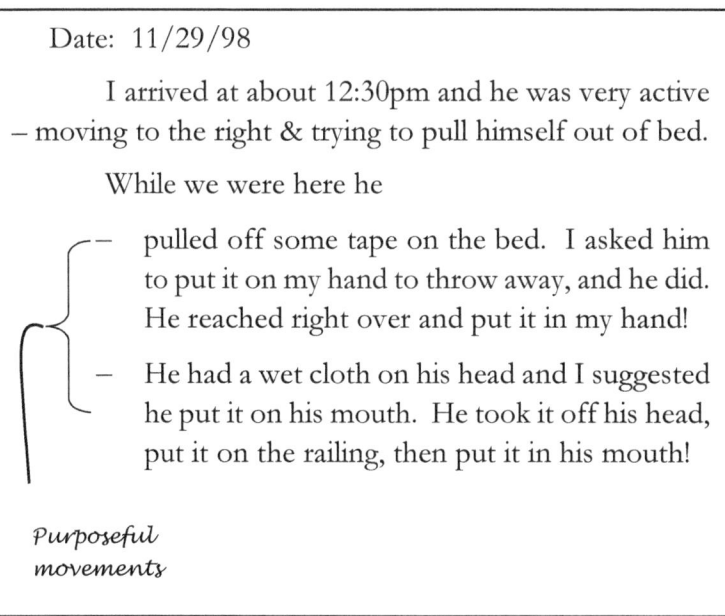

Date: 11/29/98

I arrived at about 12:30pm and he was very active – moving to the right & trying to pull himself out of bed.

While we were here he

- pulled off some tape on the bed. I asked him to put it on my hand to throw away, and he did. He reached right over and put it in my hand!

- He had a wet cloth on his head and I suggested he put it on his mouth. He took it off his head, put it on the railing, then put it in his mouth!

Purposeful movements

He slept for fifteen minutes between 1:15 and 1:30. He fell asleep about 2:10 and hadn't woken when we left at 2:30.

Please encourage the sitters to read his bio that I hung up and also put on a CD for him to listen to if it seems appropriate.

I also brought him a bag of textures he could feel.

Karen and Fred

Date: 11/29/98   Time: 3:00 pm

We (Andy, Annie, Mom) arrived and found Kevin active – turning to the right, flopping his leg over, etc. He seemed to settle down as Andy/Annie rubbed his feet while Mom wiped his brow with a cool cloth. Fell asleep for about ten minutes. The nurse said she'd call about giving him something to help him sleep tonight.

Date: 11/30/98

I arrived at 9:00am & found Kev constantly wiggling! Very active… His nurse and Jenny (his sister) informed me he will be moved to Craig Hospital this morning! His nurse gave him his A.M. medicine (antibiotics, antiseizure, etc.) He also got his regular respiratory nebulizing treatment. After that, he slept for a while. Now we can't wait for the big move!

—Dan

Chapter 2: Why am I here?

Date: 11/30/98

Jim and I (Karen) arrived around 1:30 at Craig. Kevin has been very active the whole time we've been here ('til 5pm) with some periods of about 5 – 15 minutes of rest off and on. Rubbing his legs has proved an effective method for making him rest. The nurses would like us to keep him up upright as much as possible. This is somewhat of a challenge.

I have hung Kev's "schedule" on the cabinet. They encourage visitors in the 4pm → 9pm time frame especially. The weekends are unscheduled with therapy so that's an especially important time for us to be here.

The doctor orders some new ointment for his g-tube area. They will be working on regulating bowels and bladder as well as sleep/wake cycles during his week.

Date: 12/1/98

Kev went to PT, OT, and ST this morning. During his time in OT, he raises one finger, two fingers and five fingers when asked! He followed me with his eyes when asked. With his PT he would grab for things when asked and kicked her hand with his left foot when asked.

Kev also sat up in his bed almost on his own (pushing w/ his left hand).

– Karen

Date: 12/2/98

I got here at 10:00am. He had PT from 9:30 – 10:00. They say there's some concern about stiffness in his ankles and right wrist. Anyone who's interested can learn from the PT how to massage these areas to minimize stiffness. Ask a nurse.

He didn't sleep much at all last night & has been only sleeping in little 15 – 20 minute periods today. When he's in the chair and in therapy he is pretty still and attentive.

During therapy he:

- Chose the correct colored blocks when asked and handed them to me when asked.
- Chose a circle and triangle when asked & put them in the correct places in the puzzle.
- Not as good with the square.
- He pointed to the words "yes" and "no" on a paper to answer some questions.
- He was asked to read simple sentences and point to the "yes" or "no" to answer. He seemed to do this with one sentence.

– Mom

Date: 12/5/98

Got here at 7:30pm. Kev is in the chair trying to go to the bathroom (he was given a suppository). He didn't go after ½ an hour. I'm not sure if he doesn't want to go with me sitting there with him, so I went outside to give him some privacy.

– Dan

Chapter 2: Why am I here?

Date: 12/6/98

Jen came back and Annie & I arrived in time to get in on Kev's answering questions. – Yeh! When I said "Kev, are you frustrated that we're asking you all these dumb questions?" he <u>emphatically</u> tapped "yes"!

Annie and I both got several kisses from Kev as we were leaving. ☺ He looks <u>great</u> and wants in the worst way to get out of the bed!

– Karen

Date: 12/7/98

Got here around 3:45. He was in the chair and the put him down. I rubbed his legs and feet and he fell asleep @ 4:15.

Also, Karen said that he mouthed words today!!!

– Jenny

Date: 12/8/02

Kev did great with me today.

He:

- correctly answered a physics question (one about Newton's Law
- talked a lot to me (he mouthed it) and when I couldn't understand, I wrote various options and he circled the one he wanted.
- he wrote "yes" and "mom" with his left hand
- he wanted me to ask him more simple question (rather than physics ones)

– Jenny

Starting about December 9, 1998 I find the first attempts to write that I was able to make. Someone would write out various options that I could circle the answer I most wanted. Questions about my feelings looked like this:

I wrote this about December 19, 1998

Just after that, I find in my in the log book a mention that I was able to void while sitting on the commode by myself for the first time. Then I find this scrawl to my wife:

Within a few days I start to deal with physics:

These are

(or should be)

the quantum mechanical equations

$E = \hbar\omega$

and

$p = mk$.

Chapter 2: Why am I here?

This says "God will never leave me".

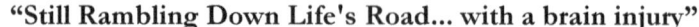 "Still Rambling Down Life's Road... with a brain injury"

CHAPTER 3
My Life As An Invalid

February 3, 1999

Recently, I've heard the term "invalid" used for people that have trouble walking. I was kind of confused about the term's exact meaning and origins, so I went to the dictionary and looked it up.

"Invalid"

The "In" means "un" or "not" like involuntary, incompressible, and inescapable. "Valid" means "correct" or "OK." So, as best as I can figure, "invalid" means "not valid," "not correct," or "not OK."

Oh, but then there's a second definition: "not able to walk."

I have problems with the use of the term "invalid." I used to be an invalid. I couldn't walk, or eat, or do anything. But was I not valid or not OK.? No!!! I was still a real person, just like a non-negligible portion of our population.

There used to be a president – was it Wilson or Roosevelt – who couldn't walk and used a wheelchair. Was the most powerful man in the world not correct or not OK.?

Apparently, there was a debate over what to call people like me. Probably there still is one. "Disabled" is the term that's been settled on. (Apparently, some disabled people felt that everyone should be called "temporarily able-bodied".) The label "handicapped" is out of vogue.

But I kind of like the term handicapped. A handicap is something that makes it (life in this case) tougher for people. Like golf. Who has the biggest handicap? The best player, like Tiger Woods. In golf people who have a larger handicap are more ready for bigger challenges. Maybe that's why some people can't walk.

Today after I had a cap put on my tooth, which had been broken in the accident, I went back to my room. Dave, my therapist, came by and we started talking. I told him about my new tooth and he went and got a hand-held mirror. He brought it to me so I could look at my tooth (the fake one). While I was doing that I noticed a relatively small bald spot on my head.

"God damned accident! Look at that God-damned bald spot. I can't believe that it's affected me in this way," I said, pissed as hell.

Dave smiled and said, "I think that's naturally occurring, Kevin."

I can't believe it! I had forgotten that I'm working on a small bald spot on my head. Oh well, you take what you're given.

Then we were practicing my handwriting again. It's really bad but it's improving, slowly. When I started trying to write again, my right side had trouble moving because of that darn clonus problem. I had to switch to writing with my left hand.

As it turns out I had some trouble writing with my left hand, too. Everything that I wrote looked like it was in a mirror. I didn't write, "This is my bed," I wrote, "deb ym si sihT." It's better now, but not perfect, and I use my right side. That's my normal side.

That makes me wonder about the cause of handedness. I don't think it is passed down in the genes. Maybe when you're young, your handedness locks in. If when you're really young and you get taught to or see people using their right hand, you become right-handed. That would explain the flexibility I seem to have.

Chapter 3: My Life As An Invalid

We were finishing up when Karen came in. I was happy to see her and glad I was almost done. To finish off, Dave had me sign my name.

He looked at it and showed it to Karen and asked her, "How's his signature look?"

Karen glanced at it and responded quickly (too quickly in my estimation).

"It looks better. Much more legible."

I was amazed because if you look at it, it actually is more legible. That is a pretty bad indictment of my writing (or signature at least) before the accident.

February 6, 1999

I was thinking about one of my speech therapists, Rachel, today. She's really nice and pretty good-looking. She helps me a lot and I'm really thankful for that. But all these thoughts got me thinking.

I think I love Rachel! A lot. That must be my feeling. It's not that I don't love Karen. I must, because we've been married since ... Oh, hell. I don't remember! But it's been a long time.

I know I love Karen and I think I love Rachel too. I must, because I can't feel much difference between my feelings for Karen or Rachel. It must be love.

February 8, 1999

Today, when I was in physical therapy, I walked with a walker to support me!!! I was so happy. Maybe it's a sign that I'll be able to walk again without any assistive devices like the walker. Or maybe I'll use a cane. We'll see.

"Still Rambling Down Life's Road... with a brain injury"

February 11, 1999

I've been practicing walking with a walker. It's OK, except at stairs. The stairs are tough because you can't really use a walker on them. You have to carry it up in your hand and can't hold on to stuff. So when I've been practicing walking up and down stairs, it has been without a walker.

I don't seem to have trouble going up stairs. If I can hold on to the railings it's OK. It's not like I jog up them, but at least I can do them. It's going down them that's tough.

When I'm going down stairs, I find it hard to keep my balance. You'd think it would be the same as when you go up stairs, but it isn't. It's a lot harder. I've been spending a fair amount of time thinking about why that is.

The physicist within me woke up with the answer. I know why that is! It's obvious. When you're going up the stairs, you're working against the force of gravity. It takes you straining your muscles to work against gravity.

When you're going down the stairs you're working with gravity. It's a kind of controlled falling. When you walk down stairs, you're trying use the force of gravity to help you, but you're trying to control it, too.

It's kind of like this cloness problem. When you're straining your muscles, no problem, you can do it. When you're trying to relax them and calm them down, big problem, it's really tough.

I guess that's the way it is with life. It's not so hard to fight against something, to struggle to make things better. But it's tough to let forces take you for a ride and push you along. It takes careful decision making and a lot of self-control, two things that are tough for me now. I wish I knew someone that sailed for fun. Sailors use a force they can't control (the wind) to their advantage. Maybe I'll be able to do that someday.

Chapter 3: My Life As An Invalid

February 12, 1999

Today I got to leave Craig!! It turns out I don't need so much help. For example, I hardly need my wheelchair anymore and mostly use my walker. Although, I did ride out of Craig in my wheelchair. I thought it would be a good ending to being at Craig – being so much like my days at Craig. I have no idea what I've got coming – maybe starting my job at Carleton, not right away but soon.

February 22, 1999

Today I started at a hospital in Boulder: Mapleton Hospital. It turns out; I didn't know it as Mapleton when I grew up. Back then it was called Memorial Hospital. I should know because I was born there! As it turns out, sometimes my therapy is about 500 feet from where I was born. Talk about coming full circle.

Today, I was wondering if problems from this accident could be passed down to any children we have. If they were just physical problems of the right sort I wouldn't worry, but brain injuries are different.

The brain controls everything. I mean the brain controls everything and everything is messed up with me. Like my heart rate: they measure it at the hospital to see if it's OK. But after they measure it and wait a minute and measure it again, it's really different – about 20 to 30 beats/minute different. The same is true with my blood pressure. It can change about 30 lbs./in2 in a minute.

So today I was worrying about any kids we might have. Does my body (which is controlled by my brain) now make messed up sperm? I'll have to ask a doctor.

Karen told me that this is the third hospital I've been at. I remember being at Craig, but I have no memory of any time before that. Apparently, I was at Hennepin County hospital in Minnesota. I remember nothing of that, and I hope it stays that way.

February 26, 1999

Today at Mapleton they switched me to a walker permanently! Walkers are so much easier to work with. They fit into cars much easier. That makes riding in a car so much easier. Riding in a car is so much easier now, but all the problems with riding in a car aren't physical – they're emotional. It's still pretty hard to sit in an automobile.

As it turns out, I was told Colorado has a pretty strict seatbelt law. You have to wear one. I think I'll never have any trouble with that law. Any time I get into any car, I feel a strong compulsion to put my seatbelt on.

CHAPTER 4

April 15, 1999

Ms. ---,

...

On October 27th you were driving down Highway 3. It has a 40 mph speed limit and you were going more than 60 mph. Not that this is an estimate, evidence shows you were going at least that fast. You ran a yellow/red and hit a virtually motionless car. Why? You must be a shitty driver.

...

"Still Rambling Down Life's Road... with a brain injury"

CHAPTER 5
Being Mentally Disabled

March 1, 1999

I switched from a walker to a cane today! Gosh, I'm glad my imprisonment in the walker didn't last for as long as my imprisonment in the wheelchair did. I hope someday soon I can get rid of the cane, too.

I figured out something the other day. I think Karen and I should write a will and keep it up to date. I think we'll have to outline different things to do depending on who's alive. If Andrew's still alive, I think he should have everything. If not... Hmmm. That's kind of unpleasant to think about such bad thoughts. I'll leave it for later.

Karen told me that, as it turns out, it was an accident and it was mostly the fault of the woman who hit us. (As I figured.) I think she must have wanted to hit us.

She did it on purpose. I know that's kind of ridiculous, but I feel that she must have wanted to hit us. Karen explained to me that we were essentially motionless at a light. The light turned yellow and someone honked at us from behind. They also must have thought it was safe to go, too.

~ "Still Rambling Down Life's Road... with a brain injury"

Apparently, some witnesses say that the light had turned red and some say it was still yellow. Anyway, we went and were run into by someone going really fast. I imagine it went like this:

It was 8:04 and R----- was late for work (she was supposed to be there at 8:00.) and she was really tired. To save the precious minutes she was driving a little bit over the speed limit.

"Gosh, I hope my boss doesn't get mad. He got really pissed last time," she thought.

Fortunately, Northfield is a small town so it will only take a few minutes to get to work.

She and her friend had been out for dinner last night and met some interesting guys. They went home and had a fun time getting to know each other and downing whiskey. She was surprised because she didn't have a headache even though she had put back her last drink a couple of hours ago. Boy, was she tired.

"This guy is so great by giving me his car. I'll have to buy him another three bottles of whiskey to make up for the ones the four of us drank. I hope it doesn't rain or snow. It looks really cloudy out there," she thought again.

She saw the clock again and decided she'd better step on the gas. It was late. She looked at her speedometer. It said only 63 mph and the speed limit had changed to 40 mph only about 2 miles ago.

"That's the way to go when it's morning and you're late," she thought.

Some distance in front of her she saw the light turn yellow. She stepped on the gas to get to work soon and made it through the light when it was a yellow light. Stepping on the gas caused her coffee to spill on her. The coffee started to pour out onto her friend's carpet. It was her friend's carpet because it was her friend's car. She looked down at the fallen cup, looked up and saw a car turning left in front of her. She slammed on the brakes for at least 0.1 seconds and DAMN she hit the car.

"What a wreck!" she thought. "Fortunately I'm not hurt at all. I really feel bad about this and I'll give them a call tonight."

Later the police arrived and started to clean up.

Chapter 5: Being Mentally Disabled ✎

"Hi R------!" the stupid officer said.

"He must remember me from a couple of months ago," she thought, angry that he used her first name.

Well, that's how I figured it happened, or something a lot like that must have happened. Whatever happened happened, there's nothing you can do about it.

March 15, 1999

I had physical therapy today. My physical therapist, Margaret, gives me a massage once a week. Most people think I'm really lucky and wish they could be like me (at least, sort of like me). But she gives me these massages to help my range of motion problem on my right arm. They aren't feel-good massages, they hurt! She apparently does some soft tissue work. They're just normal massages but much harder. She also does some bone work and moves my bones around. It's nice to have such attention paid to me. I just wish it wasn't this much attention.

Today at physical therapy Margaret measured my weight. I weighed about 205 pounds! Wow, that's a lot! Before the accident I weighed about 175 pounds. I have no memory of this (as I don't for a lot of things now) but when they checked me into Craig, I weighed 142! Talk about a painful but effective weight loss program – the accident caused me to loose over about 30 pounds in one month.

Weight must be why I had the worst injuries of anyone in my family. (The fact that a car was headed straight toward me doing about 63 mph and was about six inches from me must have had something to do with it, too.) I must have hit the walls of the car harder. This may be why males are more likely to suffer TBIs, too.

Actually, I may have hit with the same speed, it's just that it takes more force to slow so much more mass down. It's that old conservation of momentum law again. If anyone had any feeling for what it's like to have a traumatic brain injury (a TBI) and any knowledge of the conservation of momentum, they would have a strong compulsion to lose weight fast.

That must have been why my two-year-old son Andrew wasn't hurt so much. After we were hit, he was going the same velocity (about 25 mph), and then he was stopped by his car seat when we hit the traffic light pole. But if he had to stop in the same distance, he'd feel a much smaller force (about one-sixth as large.) That's why he didn't break so many bones or puncture his lungs.

My wife had one lung punctured. I had both lungs punctured by six of my ribs that were broken. My kidneys, liver, and spleen were torn, my face broken in four places, my clavicle was broken and my pelvis broken. About two months ago, one of my doctors at Craig said I was really lucky to be alive. He said that had this accident happen two years ago, I would have died. (Wow, some recent medical advances saved my life!) Our accident must have been bad. In a way though, I think that a part of me did die.

It's funny. My beard has been pretty scraggy since I was at Craig and Karen didn't like it and neither did I. As a result, I shaved a couple weeks ago. When Karen saw me, she exclaimed, "You shaved! Thank God!"

Andrew was with us and overheard her. So now each night when we're praying for dinner Andrew prays:

"Thank you, God, that daddy's feeling better. And thank you, God, that daddy shaved off his beard."

Talk about taking Karen seriously.

April 14, 1999

I started walking by myself today with no walker and no cane! I walked as part of my physical therapy. Later at dinnertime, Karen, Andrew, and I were having dinner over at her parents' house where

Chapter 5: Being Mentally Disabled

we are staying. We all sat down to dinner, and I stood up and said, "I've got an announcement. I'm done with the cane."

Then I picked up my cane and threw it across the room (really hard). That's the last I'll deal with a cane (until I get real old, if I ever get old.)

April 19, 1999

Today, we moved from Karen's parents' house where we had been living for two months. We chose to move out and get out on our own again. I am getting around much better and need less help. So we went out and found an apartment.

Before we rented it, when we were looking at the apartment, the owners were nice and said "How's the recovery going Kevin?"

"Fine," I said and I'm sure I looked pretty funny. A little bit later I asked Karen, "Are we famous. I mean famous, world famous?"

She said, "We sure are, at least in Boulder and Northfield." I laughed because I honestly thought we might be world famous.

As it turns out our new apartment is right next to another apartment for the "mentally disabled." I'm sure that when the city moved an apartment for the mentally disabled people next to ours, the estimated value of this place was affected. I'm sure it went down, maybe way down.

I have some problems with those words "mentally disabled." Are retarded people "mentally disabled"? Suppose your IQ is low, say 50. Are you "mentally disabled" then? I think "mentally disabled" is a poor set of words.

"Disabled" means "doesn't work" or "unabled." Some people, like crippled people, are really disabled. Their disability is their legs don't work. Sure enough, they're disabled.

But "mentally disabled," what does that mean? That would mean your brain doesn't work. Your brain controls everything. I mean everything. It even controls your bowels. I know because I used to go to the bathroom on myself in my bed. Why? Because my brain was messed up, and I was kind of "mentally disabled.".

But my brain was working, just not as well as it used to. It still doesn't work as well as it used to. I'm still not "mentally disabled."

I think the words "mentally disabled" are often used when the words "emotionally disturbed" would apply better. I think these words better describe our neighbors, at least.

It's kind of funny because I shared some feelings of uneasiness when I found out that they lived nearby. It must be that the difference between mentally disabled people and emotionally disturbed people has me confused, too. They've been labeled "mentally disabled" because there's no label for what they are.

I think that our language should reflect reality. The reality is that the brain functions on a wide-ranging scale. Sometimes it barely works. My brain used to be that way when I was at Craig hospital. Sometimes it works really well, like it did in Albert Einstein's case. (I hope that my brain gets back to functioning at one half or one quarter of an Einstein Level. That would be good enough for me.) But there should be a new descriptor instead of "mentally disabled." Hmmm... How about "mentally malfunctioning"?

May 15, 1999

Today, my brother Dave, his family, Karen, Andrew and I went down to the Boulder Creek festival. It was a lot of fun, so many people and so many things to do. One thing was really weird though. I felt like an alien who has never visited earth before who was beamed down onto the earth and experiencing everything for the first time. I feel like I'm entering everything unaware without any preconceptions.

Chapter 5: Being Mentally Disabled

There was this Asian woman who was wearing a bikini top and was extremely flat. I mean compared to her, Dave and I have big breasts. Not that that's a problem, but it got me thinking.

Why do women need to wear tops? Obviously it's because they're sexual organs. But why are they sexual organs? I asked Karen about this and she said it's because they're more sensitive. Why is that? Because they're usually clothed and are treated with more care, I figured. This starts the whole question over again.

At least a woman's breasts are usually used for something – feeding babies. But you'd figure that since they are actually functional they should be exposed more than men's nonfunctional breasts. Bras are much more understandable. At least they perform a needed function.

Why do men have hairy chests? You'd think that women would need to keep their milk warmer so they would grow hairy chests. You'd think kids prefer their milk warm, like a latté.

It should be men who need to wear tops. I don't understand. One thing I hope is that this outsider perspective keeps up and will apply to my work. It would be really useful in physics.

Which brings up another thing I've had questions about. I think most people who believe in God believe God is all-powerful (in a good way). After all, people believe he created the world in six days. They also believe he is all loving. If not, why should we love him? Which brings up another question. Why is God a he and not a she?

If God is all loving and all-powerful, explain World War II and the everyday murder of innocent people. Recently, there was this tragic murder of many people at Columbine High School. Why did God allow those two students who killed everyone to obtain guns? Why not just kill them? Couldn't they have dropped dead just before the incident from heart attacks? I just can't figure it out.

Oh, yeah... Today at the creek festival there was a drawing you could pay to enter. For only one dollar you could enter this game and the prize was a quarter of a million dollars! Now, I've never entered a game like this before. Why would I? You only have a one in a million chance of winning. But I felt a strong compulsion to enter. I started to think about what I'd do with my quarter of a million dollars. In my mind, I had already won.

I said to Karen "Hey, there's a drawing we need to enter. We've got to give them one dollar and buy a ticket!" I was very excited.

"No, we shouldn't enter. We'll never win," she said back.

"We've got to enter. We've got a one in a million chance of winning. I've got plans for that quarter of a million dollars." I said, more interested than ever.

"You've already beaten such odds. You're still alive," she said.

That kind of put a damper on the conversation. She's right. The chance of my living and recovering as quickly and as well as I have is truly only a few in a million. I'd attribute my recovery to the doctors, nurses, therapists, and techs that gave me my life back.

"But if I've been this lucky so far why shouldn't my luck keep going?" I wondered.

June 1, 1999

I've got a new first memory! It's way better than the memory of having a catheter stuck into your penis. It was in mid-December, about a month and a half after the accident. It turns out that the cheerleaders for the Denver Broncos came to my room! They were talking to me and cheering me up. (I had a long way to go.) I think they started coming there when a Bronco got hurt in a game and have been coming there ever since. After they were through cheering me up a bit, they got ready to leave. One of them really cheered me up. She gave me a kiss!

I was really happy today and I don't feel a need to have my memories go back any further. Any earlier than that and I'm sure any memory would be a lot worse. That's far enough.

CHAPTER 6

Here is some information I was sent by Hennepin County Medical Center:

HCMC Trauma Services
Level 1 Trauma Center

Dear Dr. David XXX,

Kevin Pettit, 31 years old, was admitted to Hennepin Count Medical Center on October 27, 1998. Mr. Pettit, his wife, and child were involved in a motor vehicle crash. Mr. Pettit was the restrained passenger in the vehicle which was T-boned on the front passenger side. His wife, Karen, was also cared for in your Emergency Department then transferred to our facility for further care. Their child was unharmed in the crash.

"Still Rambling Down Life's Road... with a brain injury"

Examination in the Northfield Hospital Emergency Department revealed a fractured clavicle, ruptured diaphragm, and closed head injury. He was intubated, C-spine, chest, and pelvis x-rays were taken, and a maintenance IV, Foley and nasal gastric tube were placed.

On arrival to our Stabilization room and 1000, General Surgery and Neurosurgery staff were present to assess the extent of his injuries. He had x-rays taken, maintenance IV continued, and Versed given for sedation. His vital signs remained stable. He was taken to the CT scan area for a head CT which revealed a subdural hematoma and subarachnoid hemorrhage. He went to the OR for an exploratory laparotomy with repair of a left hemi-diaphragm, spenic and liver lacerations, and a chest tube placement for bilateral pneumothoraces.

Mr. Pettit is currently in the Surgical Intensive Care Unit. His Glasgow Coma Score post-operatively has been 5 to 8. He has had a ventriculostomy placed for monitoring. He is listed in critical condition and is being mechanically ventilated. His family is present at the hospital and is being supported by staff. His wife Karen has been transferred to the surgical floor.

Thank you for referring this patient to Hennepin County Medical Canter for further treatment. We appreciate the excellent care he received prior to transfer. We will keep you informed of his progress and plan of care. Please feel free to contact me with any questions or concerns.

Sincerely,

Matthew XXX, MD

Department of Surgery
Hennepin County Medical Center

Dave,
Kevin is still very neurologically depressed.
I'm not sure what the outcome will be.

Matt

CHAPTER 7

Here is some information I was sent by the police:

> Supplementary Investigation Report
>
> NO: 98005502 Vehicle Accident w/ Injuries
> Classification
>
> DETAILS OF OFFENSE, PROGRESS OF INVESTIGATION, ETC.
>
> Date 10-27-98
>
> On 10-27-98 at about 0759 hrs I observed the end of a two-vehicle accident in the intersection of Hwy #3 and Jefferson Parkway. I called this in to dispatch and responded to the scene. On arrival I observed a full-size red pickup at rest in the middle of the intersection and a mid-size silver station wagon at rest against the base of the light standard. I went to the passenger side of the wagon and found an adult male, unconscious and unresponsive.

"Still Rambling Down Life's Road... with a brain injury"

The rear seat of the wagon contained an infant secured in a child seat. The child was crying and did not have any visible injuries. The driver, adult female, was being tended to by a Northfield Hospital Ambulance Paramedic. He was on his way home in his personal vehicle when he witnessed the accident. The adult female driver of the truck stepped from her vehicle and did not appear to be injured. I requested the Fire Department to bring extrication equipment and requested an additional ambulance and informed dispatch this was a code red situation.

XXX stated he was third in the left turn lane of southbound Hwy 3. The light was green and left turn traffic was waiting for northbound traffic to clear. The light changed to yellow and the silver wagon pulled into the intersection. He stated he then heard the vehicle in front of him sound its horn and then the silver wagon pulled out into the intersection in the path of the red truck. The truck then applied its brakes and he heard the tires skidding on the wet pavement. The truck was unable to stop and struck the wagon in the passenger side doors. The wagon then spun around, rear tires in the air and then went forward and hit the light pole.

CHAPTER 8

April 15, 1999

Ms. ---,

...

After you hit us my son seemed fine. But how can you tell if a two year old has a brain injury? It's not as if you can ask him to raise his right hand. The main problem I've noticed thus far is that his father was taken away from him for four months (literally) and part of him is still gone.

After the accident the emergency crew had a difficult time putting an IV into my wife's arm. If you want to know how painful it was, try puncturing your arm over and over and over.

My wife's right lung was punctured. This painful problem was remedied by a surgical procedure. Not that she could feel it, she had a local anesthetic and she was knocked unconscious by the accident.

In addition, the trauma of the accident plus dealing with everything afterward interrupted her work on her Ph.D. thesis. She was months away from a final draft.

What happened to me? Tons. I had two punctured lungs, contusions on my liver, spleen and kidneys, a right clavicle was broken in two places, my skull broken in four places, my pelvis shattered, one tooth broken, and another was moved around. Worst of all, my skull was fractured and I suffered major brain damage.

...

CHAPTER 9
God Did It

June 2, 1999

Karen told me today that after the accident I was unconscious for a long while. I was in a coma for 11 days after we were hit! Bummer. It's really lucky that I'm still alive. I was thinking about the accident today (just like every other day.) And I was having trouble comprehending why it was us who were hit. It must be that she was after us. She hit us on purpose.

No, that's ridiculous. It must be that we did something in the recent or distant past to deserve this. It must have been me; I must have done something to deserve this. That's why it was me that had the worst injuries. Hmmm... What did I do to deserve this?

It must be that God had something to do with it. Probably he was in control of this woman's car and made her hit us. (Having God in control is better than having no one in control. She certainly wasn't in control of the car.) Why else would she hit us, cause such major damage, and have no injuries?

So I'm sure it was me. It was my fault it was us who got hit. Why else would God allow this to happen? In the same vein, it must be that the people in Kosovo deserve what's happening to them. I (and they) must have done something earlier in life to make God pick on me (and them) in this way. What was it? Hmmm...

No, it isn't that we did something to deserve this. It must be that this life now is insignificant and unimportant compared the next one in heaven.

But then why all this taboo against suicide? Why didn't Jesus go around telling people to kill themselves? He wouldn't have been very popular but who needs popularity when you're the Son of God? At least that would demonstrate a firm belief in the afterlife.

Maybe it's that our life and the deservingness of salvation is judged in this life. Bad things happen to everyone to separate those good people (who respond in the right way to bad things) from those bad people (who respond in bad ways to bad things).

But isn't God smart enough to determine this without having to test us in this way? What about those people who because of the country they were born in never learn about Jesus? Are they condemned to hell just because they were born in the wrong country?

It must be something aimed at all people. If not, why are two- and one-year-old Kosovo Albanians killed?

Maybe it's payback for Jesus' death. But then, if God created the universe, why make it so horrible? Why not have little automatons walking around that could do nothing bad? It's not very hard, if you believe that God made the universe, to imagine a world where people do no wrong, bad things don't happen, and there are no accidents.

Oh, wait. Maybe it's that we're so screwed up that what we think is bad isn't *actually* bad. It's actually neutral or even good. Then if so, God would have made some pretty stupid people. Either that, or he screwed up and made a mistake when he was making people.

You'd figure that if you were God, making people would be as easy as it was to make those old snap-together models. Hmmm... No answers yet. I'll just have to keep thinking.

Chapter 9: God Did It

June 3, 1999

I heard something today from my mom. Apparently, sometime after the accident word got out that I was moving my toes and later my fingers. It wasn't as if I came out of my coma dancing, but I guess that's how they determine if you're in a coma. They prick your fingers and toes with a small pin and see if you respond in any way. One day, I guess the day I came out of the coma (11 days A.A.), I started responding to the pricks.

Looking now on my fingers and toes, I can see the scars from the pricks. On my toes, I think I can see several scars. I guess that is another way you could describe the severity of my coma. I had a six prick-scar coma.

I was watching the news today and there was more of this Clinton-Lewinski deal. What an embarrassment. Karen's sister, Janet, is a minister in Washington D.C. at the church where Clinton attends, so I had this interesting idea. If I were Janet, I would tell Bill Clinton "Repent soon or be damned to Hell!" But I guess he wouldn't find that as funny as I would.

Besides, I'm not even sure if I believe in hell anymore. I think that if I had the option, I would take existing in pain over non-existence. After a while (say a million years or so) I would start to appreciate pain and enjoy those five pain-course meals.

Which brings up another idea. Why do people see heaven as a really nice Earth? Can't existence be any different? Heaven is supposed to be nice. I love Karen and so I think we'll still be married in heaven. I enjoy making love to her. So are we going to have sex in heaven? Who knows? I figure that after a while (a couple million years or so) sex with Karen will be kind of boring. Will I move on to a new wife then?

It must be that life will be different up in heaven. We may even lose our sense of individuality. Maybe we all join into a collective consciousness – sort of like "the link" that Odo from *Star Trek: Deep Space 9* can join into. I just can't figure it out. I'll just have to keep thinking.

CHAPTER 10
What I've Learned Thus Far
(PART I)

> "Facing a fate he cannot change,
> a man may rise above himself,
> he may grow beyond himself,
> and doing so he may change himself.
> He may turn a personal tragedy into a triumph."
>
> — Victor Frankl, ***Man's Search For Meaning***

I've spent a while thinking about the accident (of course). It's been a pretty continual thought for me for about two and a half years (as long as I can remember A.A.) One of the things that I've thought a lot about is "Why me?" I don't hold my wife, who was driving the car, responsible for the decision that I get the worst injuries, and yet I still wonder "Why me?" Was it God?

For a while now, I have felt that I've come up with an answer. My answer isn't the answer, it's just an answer. There is no answer of the the type. The accident just happened. There is no answer to the question because the question doesn't make sense.

"Why?" is inquiring about the purpose for the event. It is a question that assumes that the accident happened for a purpose. It definitely happened for a reason: There was a God-dammed, terrible driver on the road who may very well have been drunk at the time. But it did not happen for a purpose.

"Why?" implies that an occurrence is forward looking and intentioned. It implies that there is a meaning behind the accident. But there is no fixed, implicit meaning behind the accident and no purpose. Hence, there is no "why."

While I firmly believe (and know) that there is no "why," I still have been beset by the question "Why me?" But the other half of my question ("me") is actually an important part of the question. It's important because I'm still here (thankfully) and it is important because it is a firm demonstration of the fact that I'm part of the question.

No, I'm not part of the question. I am the question. I am the question because it is my question. It's a question that's asked by me. But it is also a question that is asked of me.

It doesn't really matter whether or not others feel that my answer in "right." It doesn't matter because it's not an answer that is meant for anyone else or that should be useful to anyone else. To everyone else, the answer should make no sense because the question should make no sense. But to me, the answer is extremely important because the answer helps me see that the world has purpose and through it I can justify the accident.

What the answer to my "why" question gives me is a purpose. It also gives me a goal. Perhaps a useful way of rephrasing the question "Why me?" is this: "How can I use this incident to help me reach my goals? How can I use this occurrence help me become a stronger, kinder person?"

Since my recovery has gone on for so long (as recovery from TBIs usually do), I feel that I've become quite an expert on my recovery

Chapter 10: What I've Learned Thus Far...

and recoveries in general. I thought that I might help others by writing out my definition of the word "recovery".

recovery: (ri kuv' ə rē)

1. (< ME recover) The regaining of abilities lost or taken away. The return to health from sickness.

This is one of the first and most important aspects of recovery. When people are injured, they will recover – at least somewhat. Usually, it's the most basic of things and body centered, physical thing that recovers first – things like your lungs learning how to breathe again, or your heart learning how to pump again. Often, we aren't even consciously aware of the work that we do.

The important thing to remember when you're in this stage of recovery is that it is important to hold on to realistic expectations. Some parts or aspects of a person will not recover. They are lost or gone forever. This can be extremely difficult or impossible, but it is important because doing otherwise sets one up for major disappointment and frustration.

I have lost a good sense of balance. While my B.A. sense of balance was good enough that I could climb some pretty serious rock walls and perch myself comfortably on the edge of a thin rock that sits in the middle of a cliff and has a drop of several hundred feet below it, now I can't ride a bicycle comfortably, if at all. Probably, I never will be able to ride a bike comfortably. Like many aspects of recovery, balance is a very physically-based sensation that will either recover or not quite quickly.

If I had expected that a good sense of balance would be a part of recovery, that I could enjoy rock climbing again and that I would recover in this way, I would still be quite depressed. For this reason, I think it was helpful for me to have considered recovery as being over in one year. While often this is not true and recovery will go on for much longer, having this expectation made me accept those things that hadn't recovered, like my balance, and learn to live with them. It also made me more thankful of those things that continued to change for the better.

Shit happens.

We all need to learn this. We have no control over that fact and need to learn to live with our inability to control everything. This was one of the first things that I had to work to learn and to accept.

Here's a copy of a list of short notes I've kept at the ready in my day planner so whenever I look at my planner (which is several times a day) I'll be forced to run into them. The items on my list are a good measure of things I've been dealing with.

From my memory notebook:

- Be more self-conscious of my behavior.
- Work on assessment of the appropriateness of my comments.
- Bring subject back to my conversational partner.
- Listen more.

CHAPTER 11

> April 15, 1999
>
> Ms. ---,
>
> ...
>
> Time differential certainly indicates that it was your fault. How can a car going 60 mph hit one turning left going 5mph? I've tested it. It takes 3 seconds to turn left. Going 60 mph you had a minimum distance of 264 feet to react. Can't you respond in three seconds? Allowing for the rare case that you couldn't swerve at all, you'd think that you could have at least slowed down. But not if you hadn't been paying attention.
>
> ...

 "Still Rambling Down Life's Road... with a brain injury"

CHAPTER 12
I Deserved It

June 7, 1999

I don't seem to be worried about those "why" question as much any more. Why was it us who were hit? That's not so important to me any more. I think time has to wear you down. In a way, time is "a predator that stalks us all our life" like that one guy in *Star Trek* movie says. But it doesn't work against us. Things that don't matter a lot get worn down by time. Things that do matter stay fresh in our mind.

It's like this question of the existence of God. It seems to be less important now. Guess that means it doesn't matter a huge amount. I just keep going to church and it has becomes less and less important. Some things are better if you don't think about them too much.

But I have a sort of guilty feeling. Recently, I met a bunch of brain injury survivors. I know that after my accident I was worse off than these people. They told me about what happened to them and it sounds bad. They all have what is classified as a mild brain injury.

As it turns out, a "mild" traumatic brain injury (a TBI) is a diagnosis made in the first day or so after the brain injury. Moving up from "mild" there is "moderate" and then "severe." Apparently, this classification is made early on and only loosely correlates with outcome. Also, insurance companies make the classification and it basically describes how much it costs them to keep you alive.

This classification is made based on your condition shortly after the incident. "Mild" means you have a really short period of unconsciousness or always remain conscious and have post-traumatic amnesia. Your TBI is severe if you have a coma of more than 24 hours. But I was told that my coma lasted for 11 days! So what does that make my TBI? "Really severe" or "Severe x11"?

Some people with mild TBIs have difficulty with large groups of people, anxiety attacks, hypertension, difficulty with their jobs, and tons of other things – the works. But me, what still affects me? I have a little bit of problem with balance and a slight speech problem. It's called dysarthria. It still sounds like I've been drinking a lot. My worst complaint is in regards to brainpower. I imagine it will be very difficult to start teaching again. The study of physics is not for the weak of heart or people who are weak in the brain.

But compared to everything these brain-injured people have to deal with, my problems seem totally simple. Then, I always think of the "Why?" questions. Why, out of all these nice, lovable people, have I had such a great recovery? Everyone says that I had something to do with it, but I don't believe them. I just sat back passively (when I could sit) while they performed their miracles on me. Why was it me? What good things did I do to deserve this type of recovery?

Apparently, this is known as survivor's guilt. Jews who survived the concentration camps had it, too. One way to feel it is this: Suppose everyone in your family was suddenly dead and you were the only one alive. Don't you think the question "Why me?" would ever come up? You'd be happy you weren't dead. (We all should be happy.) But I imagine you'd wonder why you were spared. Any normal person would. But how are you to deal with thoughts like this?

Chapter 12: I Deserved It

I think that feelings of deserving and responsibility are very deeply ingrained in us. Andrew is just figuring out the essence of consequence. If he eats properly we say "nice job" and sometimes he has a treat. If he bangs his utensils on the table really loud like we told him not to many times, he gets a timeout. So if kids who are two or three years old start learning about deserving, it's no wonder that it becomes a part of us. If my students work really hard and spend a lot of time doing physics, they deserve a good grade. If they don't do any work and instead drink every night, they deserve an F.

But deserving is a double-edged sword. If you're doing something terrible like killing someone, you deserve to die. If you're doing something great like saving someone's life, you deserve praise. Those are pretty simple examples.

But why do some people succeed in doing terrible things without consequence? Like those two kids at Columbine High School. They succeeded in killing a bunch of people and themselves, *which is what they wanted to do*. Or why do some good people have such bad things happen to them? Who amongst the unborn children of the 60s deserved to have been Thalidomide babies?

My situation is complicated. I like to think of myself as a good person. Who doesn't? I don't think I deserved to be run into and have such terrible things happen to me. But I lived and my recovery has been really great – a lot better that many other equally good people. What did I do to deserve such a great recovery when so many other, equally good people die or have terrible disabilities?

I think I'll never believe that it's all a matter of chance. Physicist are used to finding a cause for everything. Everything has a cause. What's the cause of this accident? The only cause that I can pin down is it must be that the women who hit us was a horrible driver. I refuse to accept that it was a matter of chance.

I've had this idea for several weeks that driving cars should be put under a strong restriction like those for having or using guns. In one sense, cars are just really heavy killing and maiming machines. I don't know this for sure, but I think that more people are killed by someone using a car than by someone using a gun. Sure, people generally say it was an "accident," but I bet if people carried guns around and shot them each day, *a lot* more people would die in gun-related "accidents" each year. Sure, cars are helpful transportation devices, but they're also rolling death machines. So I think that really tight restrictions should be put on using them just as they are put on using guns.

CHAPTER 13

April 15, 1999

Ms. ---,

...

Conservation of momentum indicated that after the accident we were moving at 30 mph. More realistically (allowing for some skidding and loss of momentum) we were going 25 mph after the accident. We ran into a pole that we hit from the front. If only you had hit us from the front. Maybe the damage to the car would have been the same (totaled) but the damage to us would have been less.

...

 "Still Rambling Down Life's Road... with a brain injury"

CHAPTER 14
Surface Realities

June 10, 1999

The other day my brother-in-law Dan and I went to a restaurant named the Rainforest Café. It was really cool and had a lot of decorations (aquariums, fountains and such). There was this watery channel that had some kids playing near it. Inside the watery channel there was a crocodile!

I couldn't believe it! It was growling and opening up its mouth really far. Plus, those kids were riding on its back! I was amazed.

I said to Dan, "How can they let those kids get so near to the crocodile?"

He told me, "Hee, hee, it's fake. It's just for pretend."

Whoa, talk about confusion! That's the way I seem to be lately. I can only deal with surface truths and can't deal with anything hidden. Plus, I can only deal with one truth at a time.

"Still Rambling Down Life's Road... with a brain injury"

June 13, 1999

We are going up to Carleton for a reunion. I graduated from there in '89. We've been driving for a day and a half. It's OK., but I think it wracks my brain a bit. Driving is really tough for me. It's kind of strange. I have no memory of the accident or any bad times at Craig or Mapleton hospital. Then you wouldn't think I'd have such a strong emotional reaction to driving as I do. Someone had to tell me what happened. I must be awfully affected by thoughts then. They must be affecting my emotions more than before the accident.

Either that, or way deep down I have some memories of the accident. I hope to God that they don't ever surface in any more quantifiable terms. I don't think I'll ever feel good about driving through the Highway 3 - Jefferson Parkway intersection again. I don't think I'd mind seeing it again though, I think. I hope to be done driving soon.

I think that this trip will be very hard emotionally for Karen. She has a bunch of memories of the accident, all bad. That's why she's not going to go to my reunion. I'm glad, really glad. I even asked her not to come to Northfield, but she wanted to. I'm glad that she went to her reunion at Swarthmore College. It was like a dry run for mine. A lot of people were asking her lots of questions. I'm sure she had to answer questions like "What's up?" and "Why did you move away from Northfield?" and "How's you're family?" way too many times. It must have been like reliving the accident over and over and over 100 times. I wish that people could clue in.

CHAPTER 15

April 15, 1999

Ms. ---,

...

You can thank the Lord that I wasn't killed. It wouldn't have had to be any different for you to have killed me. If you had, I hope you would have felt terrible and had been prosecuted for murder in the first degree. You owe thanks to the police officers on the scene, doctors at Hennepin County and Craig hospital, nurses at Hennepin county, Craig, and Boulder Mapleton, techs at Hennepin county, Craig, and Boulder Mapleton. Without them I wouldn't be alive or as healthy as I am and, hopefully, you would be seriously depressed.

> Before the accident I had a reasonable belief in God. I was a "church attendee." After the accident I have a difficult time understanding how a loving, all-powerful God could create a horrible world where such shit could happen. I hope that your religious beliefs (if any) could be shaken as significantly by someone as (obviously) stupid as you.
>
> ...

CHAPTER 16
A Trip on the Dark Side

July 2, 1999

Well, today sucked. Why? I thought about it while taking a bath. Did I forget to take my antidepressant? No. The only thing I could iron out in the tub was that I must be bummed out because I don't have anything to do. Oh sure, I need to get better. But that's kind of an elusive goal. Plus, my efforts to return to "normal" living seem rather self-indulgent. Maybe now is a good, reasonable time to be self-indulgent. (I forget: how do you spell "self-indulgent", with a "g" or a "j"?) Anyway, I need to apply myself to getting better and it's so hard sometimes. Even this diary is a sort of pain. Normally, it's hard to put your thoughts down in written word. So slow… But nowadays, my writing isn't as slow as my thinking.

I think I should plan out a goal for each day, something I can aim for. What will it be for tomorrow? Hmmm… I'm going to the new aquarium in Denver. Hmm… See how things are going with my sister Annie? I'll have to think about it.

Now is a tough time because I can't rely on anyone else to set up my day. I'd be happy if therapy went 9 to 5, then my days would be planned out for me, like they were at Craig. I can't relate to the comment from a friend of my mother-in-law: "If you get tired of therapy, keep going…" If I had more therapy, I'd rejoice.

I think it's as hard as it will ever get. I can't rely on other people and I can't get into full gear because I can't handle it physically or mentally. It's not that I feel this way, but I can understand the desire to sit on my ass. I can easily understand this feeling and I'm glad I don't have it and I'm really glad that I have the support I have.

July 4, 1999

Today, Andrew and Karen were up at Winter Park with Karen's friend, D.J. Yesterday, I went to Ocean Journey with Annie and Mom and I went to *Star Wars I* with Mom. What a great movie. Apparently it's been criticized for the poor acting in it. Of course the acting is stiff. It's the first movie with so many computer-generated characters in it. Computers haven't taken acting classes yet.

I brought my tape recorder in case I wanted to tape any quotes from it. I liked a couple. One of them turned out to be "Nothing happens by accident." In my mind, I first disagreed with it. Now, I'm not sure. Certainly, my injury was an accident. But I think that if the injury can become a positive and important shaping force in my life, I will think nothing does happen by accident. I think this feeling and attitude can be really positive and gives *me* the power. It will also support my initiative to better my situation and myself.

Also another quote is by Yoda to the young Obiwan Kenobi. He says something like "Disappointment leads to sadness, sadness leads to frustration, frustration lead to anger, anger leads to hatred and hatred leads to the Dark Side." At one point I think I was on the Dark Side. I think I'm near the Dark Side now, but I hope that I'll move away from it. In the future, I hope to be only dwelling on anger.

Here's a memory note for me: Find out what cognitive state I was in right after the accident. Was I conscious? How do they know? When did I slip into a coma?

Chapter 16: A Trip on the Dark Side

July 5, 1999

Today is the day after July Fourth and my Dad is having a party. I should be there but I'm not because it's too noisy to write.

I've got two things I'd like to write about. The first is that I feel a sort of depression coming on. It can't be that I forgot my anti-depressant because I know I took it. I checked. But my depressed feelings are really pretty bad.

Last night I didn't like going to the fireworks show. When I did go, I had two anger outbursts at Karen, unfortunately. Now, my dad is having a party and I'm sitting here at Karen's parents' house doing my diary.

I think it would help if my life had some sort of goal. (I forgot to put a goal for today in my memory book.) Maybe it should generally be work or family related. Funny... work and family... that pretty much covers all my priorities. I have to remember to plan a goal for each day.

That pretty much covers it. Depression and thoughts of how to get out of it. I know this is a sort of milestone. I think that this is the first time I've had thoughts about my thinking and my feelings. I hope I get over my depression soon.

That's about it...

I just read an article about Craig Hospital. It was focused on one person who was in the Columbine massacre. It sort of pissed me off. Everyone will read it and pay attention to someone hurt at Columbine. But was there an article about me or someone similar? No. No one pays attention to the much more prevalent occurrence of injuries from car crashes caused by stupid drivers. There are more than two million TBIs per year. People need to clue into and figure out what matters and what's important.

I've noticed another thing that really frustrates me. Andrew, when he's in a good mood, is great. When he runs away from me, I can't catch up with him. When he's in a bad mood, he's terrible. He has so much energy that sometimes he turns in such a negative way. He behaves toward me in such a way as he never would have before the accident. I'm sure of this. He has even tried to strike me and pull my hair. That's what taking away the dad of a two-year-old for four months (one sixth of his life) does. I hate it. It's terrible.

July 9, 1999

Two days ago, I had an interesting thought. I had pretty good therapy sessions and then I was waiting for Karen or her mom to pick me up. I had a fair amount of time to sit there. Slowly a thought came to me. I thought that my therapists must like working with me because I'm a nice guy.

That's a big and important revelation because ever since I came out of my stupor after the accident, I've felt bad about myself. I didn't like me and I had lots of negative feeling about the accident (obviously) and me. Why me? It wasn't my fault. Even some of my behavioral problems are based on physical problems I have.

If I weren't in the accident, I'd have some ground to stand on when I say I'm a dick. I've been upset with myself often because of these emotional control problems. This is a real problem because I own my behavior and like to think that I own my emotions.

But this anger control problem is tough because accepting it involves giving up ownership of your emotions. They aren't yours – they can belong to someone else. Someone else controls your emotions and it's not you. It could be the person driving right next to you who controls your emotions.

What makes you you? Are you just a conglomeration of the experiences you've had? Are you in control of you? To what extent are you responsible for you?

Chapter 16: A Trip on the Dark Side

Apparently, many people have severe personality changes after a brain injury. Is it always bad or are some people more lovable after a brain injury? Emotions, personality, attitude, physical looks, what do you own? I think that my attitude hasn't changed but I have no idea. I asked Karen and she said some of me is the same. But all of me…?

July 10, 1999

I realized something today. I know that I used to think that I loved my therapist, Rachel. But I didn't. I have to admit that I find her pretty nice and good looking. But love? No way! I don't even know her. We talked a lot and that brought us closer together, but we always talked about me.

One of my therapists (I don't remember which one) said that this is called transference. It happens a lot with children who have been injured, and it's not uncommon in injured adults. Oh well, I think that in the car crash my whole brain got run through a blender and when it solidified (if it has already) the love part landed on Rachel. Oh well…

Another problem was that I couldn't remember what it felt like to love someone. I have to admit, I do like my therapist and she's pretty good looking. But love? No way! I think what it is… I know what it is. There's no firm event that I have to grasp onto for the feeling of love. That's like a lot of feelings that are similar and have no event for my memory to grasp on to.

The other day (when I was pretty sick with the flu or something) my mother-in-law asked me "How do you feel?" A pretty simple question and it should be a pretty simple answer.

I said, "OK, I think…"

The reason I said "I think…" is I didn't know! I felt OK. but I didn't remember what feeling good was like. (In a way, I still don't.) I felt a bit below average, averaged over my days after my accident.

But I'm not sure how good I feel. My memories of feeling good or feeling bad are lost!

See, feeling good or bad doesn't have any event that I can grasp onto. Ever since I came out of the coma and was cognisant, I know I could remember some things. But the things I can remember (especially more recent memories) need to have something firm I can remember them by.

It's like this for my son, Andrew. I always knew he was my son. I even remember being there at his birth. But I can't remember anything else about him. Sure, I know what room he slept in, in all our houses. But I can't remember anything else about him.

We are lucky enough not to have anything bad that happened to him to anchor my memories by. Unfortunately, the happy things seem not to have been important enough to anchor my memories by either.

I can't remember him teething. (In fact, I don't know if at two-and-a-half years old he is still teething or if they've all come in.) Teething, learning to walk and talk, learning to eat solid food, when he first slept by himself … they're all lost to me. It must be that they weren't important enough to plant anchors is my brain. I'll have to make sure that happy things start to plant anchors in my memory. Sadly, I also think that Andrew will never remember what his father was like before the accident.

I can remember one thing that might or might not have happened in college when I was dating Karen. There was that one girl, Jill (I think that was her name), who I spent a lot of time with. Now I can't remember if I slept with her! I can't remember doing it, but I can't remember if I didn't. Either I did sleep with her and it wasn't an event that had any memory handles that I can grasp, or I didn't sleep with her.

Chapter 16: A Trip on the Dark Side

Well, it must be that I didn't sleep with her. One would assume that having sex with someone would be a memorable event, especially if one hadn't had sex yet, like I hadn't. But that's an awfully important thing to forget and it's an awfully important conclusion to base my unproven theory of memory troubles upon.

I remember that I was a professor and I taught physics. I kind of remember preparing some overheads. But past that, I remember nothing about teaching. Nothing. I hope those memories come back, or I won't be able to do my job.

I think that memories that don't have an event to focus them – like my memories of Andrew when he was young – are tied to feelings. The feeling part of my brain is messed up pretty bad and that contributes to my memory troubles.

I know that the feeling part of my brain is pretty messed up. The other day I asked my counselor if the MRIs that were taken of me showed that the part of my brain that controls feeling was messed up. He said "No," not because the MRI didn't have enough detail, but because it's not clear from the MRI that the part that controls or feels emotions – the limbic system I think it was – was hurt any worse than the rest of my brain.

He said brain injuries come in two varieties: focal and diffuse. With focal injuries a certain part of the brain is really damaged, and you can tell pretty easily. I guess some strokes are like this. In a diffuse injury and the coma that often follows, cells from the whole brain get screwed up. I think that the buildup of fluid in the skull and the increased pressure on the brain causes this.

I had a shearing injury from my brain jiggling around and slamming against the inside of my skull. Shearing injuries are kind of focal. After I had the shearing injury, fluid started flowing to my head to help fix it. The pressure in my head built up. This caused a diffuse injury, and I think that most of my trouble is from that. It's also why they drilled a hole in my skull when I was in the emergency room – to help relieve the pressure.

Then my counselor said that it's not that it's not clear that the part of the brain that controls my emotions was messed up any worse then the rest of my brain. (Some diffuse injuries are like that.) He said that there's no physical evidence of this, but there is behavioral evidence. Apparently, my behavior demonstrates that the emotional controlling part of my brain was really hurt. Like the other day when I got really mad, cursed and left my support group. I can't even remember why I got so mad, but I did.

I think that partly explains my memory trouble of nonspecific events. I can't remember them because they're so tied into feelings. Take a pleasant event like being with a your new child or living next to the ocean for the first time in your life. Now take away all the feelings that you associate with it. Would you have any memories of it then? Would you throw the baby out with the bathwater?

CHAPTER 17

April 15, 1999

Ms. ---,

...

You can be thankful that I have as few problems now as I do: memory problems, speed of processing problems, etc.... You're to blame for reducing my IQ. Before the accident it was 147. You're probably too stupid to know, but 100 is average and the standard deviation is 15. So your hit took me from the really smart level down to 102, merely average but probably high above yours.

Will I be able to do my job? I hope so, because if I can't you'll be to blame and that will significantly increase the suit we're bringing against you. Brushing my hair, shaving my face and wiping my ass are still difficult.

The only thing that I can thank you for is the scar on my belly. It is so big I'm sure I'll win my new "largest scar" competition.

...

"Still Rambling Down Life's Road... with a brain injury"

CHAPTER 18
Acceptance= ?

July 15. 1999

The other day I saw an article in a magazine about the health benefits of forgiveness. Apparently, it benefits your health to forgive others who have hurt you. The article was about how many people have forgiven others and the benefits they feel as a result. Like this one woman who forgave this guy for killing her four kids.

In the article there was a list of things you could do to start forgiving. One of the things on the list was the idea that you should believe the person (not their actions) is a benefit to the human race.

Is R------ a benefit to the human race? Should I forgive her? Right now, it would be really difficult to do that. It's still hard for me to push through my head the idea that she didn't mean to hit us. I think that if the population of the world had been brought down to point where it was the responsibility of this woman and a guy to repopulate the earth, I'd rather see humanity go the way of the dinosaurs.

There's been a lot of talk in my support group about acceptance. Some people say it's important to accept the new you. But I disagree with them.

I'll never accept this new Kevin, his ~~emotional control~~ anger, misdirection problems or the slowness of his thinking. It's not that I don't agree that this whole accident happened. It did and it really screwed me up.

But to me, accepting this accident means giving into it and giving up on my efforts to make myself better. And if I do that, I think it will take all the wind out of my sails that is taking me on a route I like. I won't accept this accident.

But maybe accepting this accident doesn't mean ending the struggle to better myself. Should I accept it? What would that mean or change? In one sense, acceptance is pretty easy. Yes, I was in a car accident, had a severe TBI and was in a coma for 11 days. Easy, accepting reality is easy.

In another sense, acceptance is pretty hard. It means dealing with and putting up with the ramifications. My IQ went down by about a third. That's easy to admit but hard to live with. I feel that accepting all this would be like admitting defeat in the battle to make my situation better. When you see it in this light, acceptance is pretty tough and kind of bad.

But on the other hand (if there are three hands), acceptance is good. It implies not dwelling on the past and focusing instead on the future. Acceptance takes my energy off of what has passed and happened, and it ends my battle against things in the past and compels me to look into the future and what's going to happen. It urges me not to stay focused on the division line between before the accident and after the accident, and it asks me to focus on the future.

In this sense, I really should accept what has passed and it would be good (but not easy) for me accept the accident.

Accepting just means I know and realize (I accept) the best way to overcome my difficulties. In a way, it makes my struggling efforts more effective. I struggle just as much, but my struggles are aimed in such a way as to maximize their benefits and effectiveness.

Chapter 18: Acceptance=?

Accepting doesn't mean giving in, just finding and knowing the best way to fight the battle. It also means being focused on the future, not the past.

July 25, 1999

Well, I think I finally figured it out. It won't be a universally accepted solution but it's mine.

This whole question of proving the existence of God has really been bothering me. Isn't the reason people believe in God just because it placates their fear of dying? Unconsciously, they realize they have a transitory existence and rather than face that, they invent a God who gives them everlasting life.

At least they believe that God gives *some* people everlasting life, not everyone. It's obvious that many people don't deserve everlasting life. Would you want to live forever when your next-door neighbor in heaven is Saddam Hussein?

Gee, when I put it this way, peoples' belief in God is much more understandable and unfounded. Maybe I'll have to reconsider. Nah... I think I got it figured out.

Why not believe in God? The important thing is not what you believe; it's how you act. Your beliefs help you justify your actions to yourself. If they're really good thoughts, others might agree, and make them their own beliefs -- their own justifications for their actions.

What's the point of going to church then? If you act just the same way after going to church, there is none.

Everyone knows that human beings are weak creatures. They do stuff that they later regret. Humans get lazy. The point of church and the belief in God is that it helps keep one headed in the right direction. It should and often does help one stay working hard on the things that matter: environmental strength, diversity, and interactions and love between people.

In the past and even today a number of people were and are misguided. Slavery, hatred of Jews in WWII, and to this day, hatred of gays – they were and are evil things. Who, except someone as stupid and lazy as Pat Robertson, has a problem with gays? It's like someone being against blond haired people marrying black haired people. What matters is objectifying people as sexual objects. Last time I checked, some heterosexuals did that and some homosexuals did that, too.

When bad things were done with the church as an excuse it was even worse. Like the Crusades. Someone must have benefited monetarily and that's why they supported them. They should have never happened. God was against them. At least the God I believe in was against them. Christian, Jewish, Taoist, Muslim, … who cares?

Paul said something like this in Galatians. "In Christ there is neither Jew nor Greek, there is neither slave nor free, there is neither male nor female: for you are all one in Christ Jesus." Doesn't being one also apply to religions?

At the time that Paul was writing it wouldn't have made sense to write "in Christ there is neither Christian or Buddhist…" But wasn't that his point? To the people to whom he was writing, you couldn't get more different than Jew and Greek. The difference now is that there are a lot more people that we know of; the human family circle is a lot bigger.

What matters is how you act. To the extent that a religion gives you the strength to rise up above the fray and live a good life – treating people with love and respect – to that extent, a religion is good and worth believing.

What's the importance of going to church? It's important and it's the right thing to do if it challenges you to rise above the temptations of your weaker side and helps you act in a good way.

Chapter 18: Acceptance=?

I think it is best to go to church with your brain *on* and *working*. Church is a good time when you can think about your life, the meaning of it, and the importance of getting the *important* things right. I think people, being people, let their brains relax when they get to church. No one should let that happen. No one is good enough for that.

I've got this great *Star Trek*-like image of an entity existing because millions of people for millions of years have poured their hearts and souls into him. Can this be the way it is with God and can such a thing actually happen? Who knows? Who understands the origin of the beauty of life anyway? Can my *Star Trek* image be the way it is with God? Why not? life (plant, animal, and human) is such a mystery and a blessing.

Suppose you believed God and all this was wrong? It wouldn't matter if you have lived a better life having believed (with your head on) in this way.

July 27, 1999

Whoa, I made a mistake for several months! I thought owning and driving cars should have the same restrictions as owning and using guns. I actually thought there was a restriction on owing and using guns! Wow, was I confused, or what?

Of course, there is a restriction on using cars not guns. You have to have a license and be at least sixteen to drive. But you could be six to legally use a gun. I think I shot my guns with my dad when I was a kid (probably 12 years old).

I don't see why you have to have a license to drive those killing machines called cars but don't need to have a license to use those killing machines called guns. Now, probably this is a dumb idea of someone with a brain injury, but I think we ought to have a law that says that you need to take some class (call it a Gun Owners' Education class) and have a license before you can legally shoot a gun. I bet that would cut down on those gun related "accidents" otherwise known as murders.

That brings up another point. So you've been to the bar or were at home and had several drinks. You get in the car to drive somewhere and are pulled over by a police officer. You might get a drunk driving arrest, but what does that mean? A fine or a suspension of your license for a short time or something small like that? I think it should be much bigger.

If you're arrested for drunk driving, they should prosecute you for attempted murder. Now, I know that people who kill others in a driving accident usually don't mean to do it, but by neglecting the motive that's one way you can see drunk driving: attempted murder.

If you were drunk and shot a gun off in town "accidentally" and killed someone, you'd be prosecuted for attempted murder. But driving when you're drunk? It's the same result: death. It ought to have the same consequences.

CHAPTER 19

April 15, 1999

Ms. ---,

...

You probably feel fine now and consider this "accident" as one of those things that happens, or you consider it our own fault. You'd be completely wrong. I'm aware that you have a horrible driving record. I know you've been arrested twice for drunk driving. You are lucky that the police didn't test you for drunkenness at the scene of the crime.

It's not often that you can find someone as blessed with intelligence as I was to run into. It's also not frequent that you find someone who has a family as lovable as mine to run into and practically destroy. I'm sure this terrible accident was completely your fault. Don't feel OK. or fine about this. You have destroyed part of our lives and earned the ~~hatred~~ anger of a number of nice, loving people. I hope you rot ~~in hell~~ on the dark side.

Sincerely and with the greatest ~~hatred~~ anger,

Kevin Pettit

CHAPTER 20
Nothing Happens by Accident

July 30, 1999

I went to see the new *Star Wars* movie today. It was actually the third time I've seen it. I keep going back to see it because it's real moving, especially a couple of parts. I wanted to remember the parts I like so much so I brought my hand held tape recorder so I could record those parts and use it to help me remember them. After I saw it, I got an idea that I ought to write a letter to George Lucas to tell him how moving I found it and thank him for making it. So I did. Here it is…

"Still Rambling Down Life's Road... with a brain injury"

July 30, 1999

Dear Mr. Lucas,

I would like to tell you how much I enjoyed your movie, *Star Wars I: Phantom Menace*, and a little bit about how it affected me very strongly and positively.

I used to be a professor of physics at Carleton College in Northfield, Minnesota. Last October, a woman driving another car hit my wife, 2-year-old son, and me. It was entirely her fault, not ours. Fortunately, my son wasn't hurt and my wife only had a punctured lung. I was in really bad shape.

I was in a coma for 11 days, had physical injuries too numerous to describe, and had a major brain injury. I was in ICU for a month, an inpatient in another hospital for three months, and am now doing outpatient work at a third hospital. I have had an amazing recovery, but I still have a number of problems. But at least I am able to walk now.

Quite recently I went to the *Star Wars* I movie and was strongly affected by it. The part I liked the most was when Qui-Jon Jinn says something like "Nothing happens by accident..." On the surface this statement is complete crap. I am a prime example of how accidents can happen. But underneath (and I think this was his point) it puts the ball in my court.

Chapter 20: Nothing Happens by Accident

> I shouldn't be moping around feeling sorry for myself. I think the attitude expressed by the quote means that I have in this next year (which will be taken not by my job but by rehabilitation therapy) a chance to improve my life.
>
> I will have one year to strengthen my marriage (which was already going fine), write a physics textbook, and help others with disabilities. I think seeing the movie opened my eyes to something very important.
>
> The movie helped me greatly at this time when I need so much help. I wanted to share with you the positive way that I was affected by your work and tell you how much it meant to me.
>
> I hope you get a chance to read this and everything is going well for you.
>
> Thanks a lot,
>
> *Kevin Pettit*
>
> Kevin Pettit

"Still Rambling Down Life's Road... with a brain injury"

CHAPTER 21
Life's a Labyrinth

August 10, 1999

It was interesting. As part of this morning's activity at church camp (where I am now) the adults learned and experienced a labyrinth. It turns out a labyrinth has been an important part of many religious traditions since the Middle Ages. They symbolize the journey of life.

They aren't mazes. You never get to a point where you have to decide anything. There aren't any options or decisions, just a strange and circuitous path. And there aren't any ends or ways out, only in. At the "end" (if it is an end) is a place to sit and contemplate, relax and learn. To get out, you need to go back the way you came in.

I think that it represents our lives, since there aren't several journeys, just the one *big* journey. In our lives there are numerous sub-journeys, all part of the big journey. We learn on each of them. Maybe this accident was just a small bump on the big journey.

This labyrinth was a replica of the Chartres Cathedral labyrinth. While I was walking I remembered that I've been to Chartres cathedral. My high school choir sang there on our European tour.

While walking I realized how important the anti-mazeness was. There were no decisions – no choices – that had to be made.

Everything just led onward. That's important because it mimics what a good spiritual life should be like. There aren't any decisions to be made in a grounded spiritual life. That's one thing that spirituality should be – grounding. It is a place you can jump off of to gain greater things spiritually and emotionally.

Just because there aren't any decisions doesn't mean it's simple. The length can be tough. It's not that I had any difficulty walking it today as I used to. The length of a labyrinth done correctly is tough for people in touch with their inner-selves and their inner-needs. A labyrinth is a mind exercise as much as a physical exercise. It involves deep thinking about your experiences and your spiritual journey.

Everyone has a spirit and a spiritual journey. Disagreement about the spirit and the spiritual journey comes from being in touch or out of touch with the spiritual side of you. The spiritual side of you is the part of you that's in touch with life. It's the nonphysical part of everyone.

It would be a good idea to build a labyrinth on real hilly ground so there are ups and downs. But maybe there's no need for physical representations. Maybe it should be a mental and spiritual journey just like life itself.

One interesting thing is this idea of movement. What are labyrinths like for people who can't walk? They're still on journeys so, in a way, they're still walking a labyrinth. The image if a labyrinth is an easy way for those who walk to represent a spiritual journey.

In a way, I can think of those who can walk as physically unchallenged. They don't deal with some of the hard things – the physical challenges – that the physically or mentally challenged (the "disabled") others do. In a way, you can see those who walk as not up to the challenges that some others are ready for. Maybe, that's why some people are physically challenged. Physically challenged people don't have many things to rely on and have to deal with lots of big challenges. Dealing with all this it can make them stronger spiritually.

Chapter 21: Life's a Labyrinth

In a strange way, I think this accident was a gift from God. Admittedly, a tough one, but perhaps it was a gift anyway. Maybe it was a wake-up call telling my family to take a look at our lives. Maybe we were starting down the road to a patterned, mundane life. Maybe it was a wake-up call telling us to take a good look at our lives and where they were headed.

My family certainly has been looking at our lives. Maybe it's good to sit back and take a look at where you're headed. Maybe there's something out there we're unaware of.

August 11, 1999

I feel like a jerk. I do a lot of terrible things and that makes me feel bad about myself. Like a couple of weeks ago, I went with Karen's dad and Andrew to a new aquarium in Denver. We had eaten lunch and Frank went to get us some dessert. He got Andrew some pie, himself some ice cream, and he got me some ice cream too, but he made a big mistake. He got me the wrong flavor! I got really pissed off and mad at him for getting me vanilla instead of chocolate! Now, that's an example of something that I occasionally do.

Another example would be that I threw a chair at Karen a couple of weeks ago. It was one of our dining room chairs and was big. I broke it. That makes me mad at myself. Another thing that makes me mad is I can't even remember what it was that pissed me off.

There's nothing consistent that occurs before events like this, and I can't figure out what causes them. I guess I have a major anger misdirection problem (or possibly it could be called an emotional control problem).

Maybe it is all because the "new me" is a real dick. What a jerk I am. It's really hard when you're as pissed off at yourself as I am. When I'm in bad moods, I can't find a single thing that is going well for me. I have a really good marriage, but I'm screwing it all up. I'm probably messing up my son, Andrew too.

Oh, sure. I should be happy to be alive, but I doubt even that sometimes. If I had been killed in the accident, I would have never known it. I wouldn't have to live through all the pain that I'm feeling now.

But it hasn't been all pain.

I smile whenever I see a child of Andrew's age. Playing with Andrew is wonderful fun and being with Karen is great. Oh well, I don't understand. I still feel like the "new me" must be a real jerk, though.

August 12, 1999

Well, I had a tough counseling session with my counselor the other day. We discussed some things that are still wrong with me. I apparently have anosognosia, which is this problem where you deny medical problems that you have. That got me thinking... What medical problems have I got? Some are pretty obvious though not as easy to see as a wheelchair. I can walk now, but what brain problems have I got?

I know that I used to have anosognosia. I remember that I had determined that I should leave Craig Hospital by December 20 and get back to my job teaching. That was totally unreasonable, but at the time I didn't think so.

So my counselor and I talked about anosognosia for a while. It was funny because (at the time) I refused to accept the idea that I have it or ever had it. I guess that's one of the hallmarks of this thing: denial that certain things are wrong with you or even that you have anosognosia.

He gave me an article on anosognosia. It explains what it is and how severe it can be. It makes an example of this guy who apparently lost an arm in an accident. He had one of those plastic deals as an arm. He kept complaining to his counselor that his aunt's arm (just

Chapter 21: Life's a Labyrinth

the arm) was beating him at night! That's a really, really bad case in which anosognosia is compounded by irrational thoughts.

At least I'm not having such an extreme case. At least I think so, but how can you be sure of it? What's to say I'm not a raving lunatic because of this accident? That's one of the many problems with this type of injury. It affects the most important part of your body. Everything else can be replaced or dealt with (At least I think so. Can't the heart be replaced?) But not the brain. No one, (not even people as dumb as the woman who hit us) can live without a brain. The saying "Have you lost your mind?" is taking on a whole new meaning.

So I was pretty depressed after my meeting with my counselor today. This is what I got from it. (Now I know I'm reading tons into this. But don't we all read into everything? We extrapolate a meaning from a collection of sounds or scribbles.)

At one point, my counselor said that I might not be feeling as if I have anosognosia now, but I will in the future. That's one thing that bummed me out. What am I refusing to accept now? What's wrong with me? I think it would be good for everyone to sit down and think about what problems they're having – things that are troubling them or affecting their behavior that they haven't thought about.

I've been concerned because brain injuries are so difficult to nail down. You may look fine but act without reason, say mean things to the ones you love (as I have), and act totally stupidly (like get angry for getting vanilla ice cream rather than chocolate).

But all those things are hard to see. I was concerned because I figured that when I show up in court my injuries wouldn't be obvious. The judge would say to himself, "Yeah, he had an injury, but he looks fine and doesn't look like he deserves any money."

But my counselor said that type of thing wouldn't happen. He said that my lawyer would sit me up and ask me a few questions. After answering them, my responses would make my injuries obvious. Apparently, I don't look injured, but my responses make my injuries obvious!

At least that's what I remember, but maybe I can't remember properly anymore. I know my memory is bad, but I don't think my brain is filled with false memories – it's just that I can't store as much as I used to be able to.

CHAPTER 22
Life, Love, and Killing Bugs

August 21, 1999

The other day, we went down to the mall and went to an Asian Festival. There were some interesting things to look at but primarily it was the Asian Festival of Money Making. Some things were on display, and a lot was for sale.

We watched this Kung Fu demonstration, which was kind of funny. This guy went up and took a strong looking stance with his arms out. Two other guys had long 10-foot sticks that were two inches in diameter. They swung them at his arms and they were supposed to break on him. One did. The second one had to be swung and swung and swung, but it never broke. He put his arms together in a ceremonial fashion, bowed and the other guy stopped swinging. *"Hunh... Wood is stronger than arm today!"*

Then the two guys swung two boards at this guys legs that broke on his legs. No problem, no pain.

Then one guy took a pole to his stomach. Again, the boards didn't break. This wasn't because his stomach was flabby; it was that *"Hunh... Wood stronger than stomach today!"*

After he got done, he lay down and his teammates gathered around him. Why did he do this? He must have gone through so much pain because he had been given an award that day. His teacher picked him out for the "Guy with the Lowest IQ" award.

After he got up and could hobble away, the dancing we came to see started. It was nice (and kind of sexual) Indian dancing. I had an interesting feeling: revulsion.

Why? Well, the dancing was just like all the Indian dancing I've seen – old. It doesn't look like it was done in the 50^s or 60^s but about a hundred years ago. Now, I'm no India expert, but I've never seen anything that's new. It's always old.

It's interesting. I think, as part of the recovery process, I'm loosing the oneness of my interest. But I still have it sometimes. A while ago, I would get really interested in one thing, *really* interested. It would dominate my thinking and conversations. Why? Well, I think it was because my mind can't handle more than one thought at a time.

It was like this with the Indian dancing and my feelings of revulsion. Strong feelings like that are something sort of new. I'm sure that I didn't have a problem with dancing like that before the accident. Before the accident I could probably intelligently discuss India's wonderful history and I'd have thought they were reveling in the celebration of their wonderful history. But I know I wouldn't have had feelings of revulsion like I did.

It's strange. One of the things I must be dealing with is a brain schism. Probably, part of my brain always feels that India, as a culture, celebrates in its past. Part of my brain is astounded at India's rich tradition. Part of my brain hasn't been exposed to modern Indian culture. But, now, these parts don't communicate. Either that, or they don't communicate as effectively as they once did. Before the accident all the parts of my brain spoke the same language. But now?

Chapter 22: Life, Love, and Killing Bugs

August 22, 1999

Since the accident I've become a "bug killer." Bugs that land on me or that crawl near me are squashed. Sometimes I even go out of my way to find them and kill them.

It's funny. At the rate I kill bugs you'd think the bugs would have a big conference about ways to stay away from me. They'd all have small name tags they kept on their thoraxes (or whatever that place is called) that says "Hi, I'm Ant." Boy, that would get old.

My penchant for killing bugs reminds me of how my doctors are careful to make sure that I don't develop any bad habits. They make real sure I don't drink alcohol or caffeine because it's very common for people with TBIs to develop addictions.

Like a while ago I went on a raft trip with a bunch of TBI survivors down the Colorado River. We did about a 3 – 4 hour bus ride to get to the put-in. On the bus ride there, we stopped four times to get coffee. When we were done and drove back, we stopped five times get coffee. Wow, talk about a coffee addiction!

It turns out I don't drink alcohol anymore and caffeine is no problem. But I do think I am addicted to killing bugs.

My fascination with killing bugs is definitely A.A.. After-Accident, that's how I measure time now. We're about 301 days A.A. Why do I do it?

It must be a way for me to claim control over life. It's not that I'm interested in killing larger animals like cows, ducks, or rabbits. I'm actually a little bit turned off by eating them. But in killing bugs I gain control over life.

It's not that I'm gaining control over *my* life. I wish I was, but it's like when I was wrestling in high school. Sometimes, you'd beat losers and would need to have a broken arm or leg to make wrestling them a challenge. Beating them makes you feel good. You're ready for better opponents. By killing bugs I feel that I'm gaining control over life, not my life but *life*.

It's interesting to have this feeling of losing control over your own life. How can you control your life if anyone can take it away instantly? You can control yourself more: your feelings, thoughts, and actions. Or you can seek to control the actions of other people. I think that's what drives a lot of people like presidents of big corporations or presidents of the country. They feel a need to control life, so to do that they control the actions of other people. But do they control their own feelings and actions? Not Bill Clinton.

But controlling actions leaves you feeling empty. That's why presidents are driven. They want to control life.

How do you gain the ability to control life? It must be in three ways. Most adults have control over bringing people into the world. The desire to control life must be at the root of the desire to have sex. Also, the desire to control life must be why really deranged people kill others. But they only gain control over their victim's life, not life. That's why its perpetrators feel so empty.

I get a related feeling when I kill bugs. I don't gain control over life, just the lives of those tiny bugs. That must be why I feel the need to keep doing it.

The only way to gain ~~control over life~~ (not control over life – partnership with life) is to have a kid. You rely on life to use you to propagate another and you use life so you can get another. What a great partnership.

August 23, 1999
302 Days A.A.

I'm teaching a recitation section at CU. Today was my first recitation section for the class I'm helping with. It went well. The teaching assistant whom I'm helping, John, introduced me and I was glad of that. If I had to introduce myself, I might have gone on and on about the accident like I used to. I guess I'm getting over that.

Chapter 22: Life, Love, and Killing Bugs

While I was coming back from class, I got this idea. I should see this accident in a positive way not a negative way. Of course, some of it will always be negative, but I think I can see that some of the effects on me have made me a better person.

One of these things (strangely enough) is my memory problem.

How can my memory problem affect me positively? Well, it goes like this. My memory is bad. I have lots of trouble remembering names. Today, even though I've been there many times, I had trouble finding the recitation room I was teaching in! I had to write down the room number so I will be able to find it again.

I think that as a result of my memory problems I tend to focus on the immediate more. I can't put things off until later times because I can't remember to do them. If I'm working, and want help on something now, I'll need to ask for help now because I'll forget to do it later. Do I want to do something now? I'd better do it right now or I'll forget that I need or want to do it later. If we are talking and you make a point, I'll respond to it immediately and not wait until later. Why? Because I need to respond now so I can remember what I am feeling and want to say.

I'm more of a *now* person. I live more *immediately*. So, in a way, I'm kind of thankful that this accident happened. I think as a result of the accident I have more presentness.

August 29, 1999

308 Days A.A.

I congratulated my counselor today. (I put "my counselor" because after seeing him once a week for seven months I'm not sure of his name. It's probably Mike, although it could be Mark. Nah... Mike.) The reason I congratulated him is that he is so compassionate.

He runs my support group. At the beginning of each group we go around the table and tell about our week. It's like asking this:

"Who had the shittiest week?" You get a lot of really depressing answers. But I'm amazed at the amount of compassion in him.

Compassion is caring and liking, and I believe it to be part of love. It's not that compassion, caring, and liking are the same as love. But they stem from love. They aren't given or developed in abundance. You only get so much love and you can parcel it out as you see fit: great love for a few people, lots of compassion for lots of people, etc...

If I lead my support group and gave out so much compassion as my counselor, I'd be all loved out. Either that or having such compassion would hone me like a love blade -- really sharp. (Jesus was probably a love razor blade.) Either that or Mike's a really good actor doing a great job. It must be that by loving others, you hone yourself as a love blade.

Love, like life, must be one of those ethereal things. The more you give to Love by giving others more love, compassion, friendship, etc... the more Love gives to you. We should all give to Love so it keeps giving love back to us.

Life and Love don't die. They move on as ethereal spirits. life always lives. How can we join with life and make ourselves, or part of ourselves, immortal? In doing so, we should go on, or part of us should go on, as more than just a nice memory. Memories die.

But we can live on and make life and Love stronger by joining them and by doing more than just passing them on? We should give our strength to them, pass them on, and help them grow and expand. That will insure that we remain vital parts of life and Love and that life and Love are vitally active.

CHAPTER 23
What I've Learned Thus Far
(PART II)

Mining the Soul

I mine my soul with spiritual pick and ax
searching for the golden vein.
Inside is dark and warm but all around
is bright, clear and crisp.

Your rains and your sun shower us with life and love.
Mirror lakes reflect the soaring falcons high above.
But I, like dark ash, absorb the light you send.
So, I dig deeper, hauling out the waste-rock,
and seeking the true ore.

The wisdom of your heart enlightens the hungry.
The song of your love rings out over
the pregnant fields of barley.
The beating of your heart energizes those who labor.
But in me all is dark.

Lord, have mercy on me and clear my soul
that I might discover your vein inside myself.

by Kevin Pettit, October 20, 1994

recovery: (ri kuv' ə rē)

1. (< ME recover) The regaining of abilities lost or taken away or restoration or return

2. to health from sickness.

3. (< MF recover) (a) A return to a normal condition. The return toward normal of a particular cell, tissue, or organism after a condition of misfortune. (b) To reapply a material to something. To insulate again or repaint something.

December 4, 2001

Some people are quite opposed to the use of the word "recovery" since they see it as meaning "gaining back what was lost." While recovery does usually happen – at least in part – the fact that some things are lost and will never be gained back is hard to accept. Thus, some people use the word "recovering" as a sort of lie and a pill to help them get through the hard times.

While seeing the word in that light is sometimes useful, you don't want to use it to generate false expectations. But even in spite of the reality that often the "recovering" is seen in that way, I see it differently and in a way that I think is more helpful.

"Recovering" means exactly what it saying "re – covering" or "covering again." After the accident had occurred and my coma was finished, living was still a struggle. My personhood had been stripped of all its padding, fine adornments, and what makes me an interesting and lovable person. The life force had been stripped of all it coverings.

Why didn't my life just pass away and the living, coordinated, organizational energy structures die? Because a life force was still alive in me and chose to manifest itself within me rather than pass on to another.

Chapter 23: What I've Learned Thus Far...

We all are reservoirs of life force. Even mold contains some life force. That's why mold doesn't go away even though we wash and wash and apply toxic chemicals to kill it. Apparently, even mold contains some life force that always forces it to strive for existence. That's one way to view life force: It's the continual (and very occasionally unwanted) striving for existence.

But the life force within me was unwilling to pass on and that's why I lived. In essence that's all I was just after the coma – the struggle of existence. Soon I was conscious, but my life force wasn't done. Then I spoke. But I still wasn't aware. Then I walked. As I gained mobility and the ability to organize thoughts into a coherent whole, and as I gained awareness, I was recovering. I was covering again the raw struggle for existence with abilities. I was padding my existence with thoughts and gaining the fine adornments of constructive intentions. I was re-covering my life force.

All this is hard to do, but every cell within me just had to do it. I'm sure that it was not easy to live with me while I was re-covering. I had very rough edges and some sharp points. I'm sure that my bare and raw life force pricked my family a lot.

I think that as I am today, I'm pretty well re-covered. But who knows how far it will go? I look forward to the days ahead and seeing how well re-covered I will get. But I hope not to lose my close connection to the life force within me. Since I feel it so closely I can be of more help for others dealing with the life force within them.

From my memory notebook:

– Spend less time thinking and FEEL MORE.

– Always try to take others' perspective.

– Don't let my brain race around. Live in the moment.

– Look for the BIG PICTURE in everything.

– Be more Christ-like everyday.

CHAPTER 24
I'm a Good Person

September 1, 1999

311 Days A.A.

I just got done talking to my speech/cognitive therapist. I saw her in the hallway and she commented on the Star Trek book I was reading. In response, I told her why I was reading a Star Trek book and that got me started on telling her how I used to watch Star Trek for six hours a day at Craig Hospital. I watched each movie about 20 to 30 times. I was telling her how I was told my sister, Nan, when she was leaving me at the hospital in Minnesota, lifted my arm, pressed her hand against mine, and said "Peace, Long life," just like the Star Trek character Spock does.

She needed to hurry and I wasn't catching on. She kept looking elsewhere because she had a patient evaluation coming up. Her inattention was kind of frustrating me.

Briefly, she mentioned that I was being too talkative and not attentive to her situation. That was all true. We have been working on this sort of skill for a while now. The problem was that I took it (and have taken it when others have said similar things) like she was saying that I was too open and should be more closed. That's what I've felt that my wife Karen has been saying recently.

It's not that I'm so into what I'm saying. It's not that it's impossible for me to get obvious signals from others. The hard part is talking and taking another's perspective at the same time. I think that is a hallmark of brain injury: not being able to do as many things simultaneously.

Talkativeness and openness aren't exactly the same thing. They're like the differences between quantity and quality. Depending on the situation, you may want quantity. But I think quality is always better.

Almost always. You don't want to be so talkative about everything with everyone. Some people don't deserve that much. You need to pick and choose whom to share what with. Recently, my support group was saying the same thing. I was frustrated because they said,

"Tell us what happened to you. Tell us your feelings."

I thought they were demanding that I be more open with them and I didn't feel like it. But maybe they were trying to tell me not to go off on tangents and talk too much. Probably they had a problem with my quantity not my quality.

But I know what they said. They criticized my quality, not my quantity and it hurt. Maybe they didn't communicate what they wanted to. Now, that's one thing that's common to all brain injuries – not communicating what you want to communicate very well.

But I still think they have a problem with my professor mode and way of thinking. I work in the mode where you take you personal experiences and extrapolate what you've learned from them on to everyone. That's part of what professors do. Oh well... we'll see if I become less professor-like.

September 5, 1999

315 Days A.A.

I'm still having trouble with this idea that I have anosognosia. The reason I'm having trouble is this:

Chapter 24: I'm a Good Person

Suppose I actually have this affliction (as I'm sure I once did). Then I'm not aware of, and can't be made aware of, things that still afflict me. I'd like to think I live in a more rational state.

I've been told it takes two to five years for the brain to heal itself. If I don't have anosognosia still, then my recovery is going faster than expected. Well, then maybe I'm done with my recovery. This is as good as I'll ever get. If I've still got it, that's a bummer too. Either option bums me out.

Interesting, "bums me out" used to mean so much less. I think it now means about two orders of magnitude more than it did before the accident (B.A.). That, plus my "bummed out" periods come more frequently and last longer than they ever had before the accident.

But what if, as part of this anosognosia, I don't realize how bad I've got it, how bad my life is, and all the shit that happened to me? When I finally wake up and have real bad coffee to smell, it will be terrible.

It's not as if I'm unaware that I have some problems. I have speed of processing problems, and my thinking is quite slow – not a good attribute for a physics professor. I have a hard time with my memory problems. I get mad if I get the wrong flavor of ice cream; so, I have anger misdirection and emotional control problems. I've got these problems and others, too.

For example, yesterday when I was having trouble with a homework problem for the class I help teach. It was a multi-step problem that would probably have taken me one minute before. I spent half an hour on it because of speed of processing problems. The problem that when I was figuring it out, I'd get half the way done and forget the first half of the problem. I also had problems pushing the calculator buttons correctly.

I also have trouble doing more than one thing at once. By brain is having trouble multitasking. Like the other day when I was talking to my speech therapist when she needed to go – I'm sure that I could have realized her needs. But realize her needs *and* tell a story? I can't do it now. Will I ever be able to? Who knows?

So what if I have this anosognosia thing? Then it's impossible for me to see how bad life is and how bad I am now. It's not a pleasant thought. Mom doesn't see that I have any major problems that I'm unaware of. (At least, that's what I think she said. But maybe my memory, which I know doesn't work well, remembers inaccurately or forgets some negative things.)

So if I haven't got it then my recovery is going much better than expected -- really fast. So, if I'm recovering fast and the useful timetables don't apply, then maybe I've already recovered fully. Maybe the two-to-five-year thing doesn't apply. Maybe this is as good as I'll get.

I've come up with an answer, at least an answer that I'm happy with. No one fully understands my situation, not the doctors, therapists, my family members, or me. No one knows what's going to happen to me or when my recovery will stop.

So I should do things that will help me get better, better now not later. No one knows what will happen. We all have to do what we can to get ready for what we think and hope will happen. But we shouldn't do anything that will drag us down.

October 5, 1999

343 Days A.A.

I found out something the other day. My family was eating with my aunt from Grand Junction before my younger brother's senior recital. My Uncle Bob was telling us about a program heard on an NPR radio station on the drive over from Grand Junction. The radio news program had a story on some studies scientists have done of the brain.

Using MRI, they've looked at how the brain develops as you grow. They've studied several teenagers and young adults whose brains

Chapter 24: I'm a Good Person

were normal (not kids who are among the more than 2% of people with recent brain injuries.) Now, they focused on two parts of the brain, one part that feels the emotions and one part that controls the input from the feeling part – the controlling part. These two parts are connected by two smallish "gates" that govern their communication.

In teenagers the part of the brain that feels emotion most strongly develops a lot. Maybe, as a result, you feel emotions more strongly. But your emotion-controlling part lags behind in its development. It doesn't have its growth spurt until late teens or early twenties, just before the brain ceases to develop.

This lagging behind of the growth and development of the emotional-controlling part and the tremendous development of the emotion feeling part of the brain in the teenage years has broad ramifications. I guess it sort of explains the teenage years – that and the raging hormones.

Interesting ... maybe my problem with my emotional control and my lack of feelings is related to some problem physical problem my "gates" are having. It's not that the "new me" is a dick. It's just a physical problem in my brain.

October 21, 1999

359 Days A.A.

Wow! I finally had it! Today, I had to walk across CU campus to walk home. As I was walking across campus, between all the nice buildings and past the library, and thinking about all the good that universities and colleges do, I had an interesting, strong, and happy feeling. I felt proud to teach and felt good about myself! Wow, it's been a long time since I've felt such strong, happy feelings.

I'm sure B.A. I always had such good feelings. But there was a lot of feelings on top of them and weren't on the surface so much. But this is sort of happy feeling is kind of new to me A.A..

After enjoying those feelings, this idea kind of came to me. (Probably, my therapists have told me over and over, but it never sank in.) The "new me" isn't a dick or a jerk. The anger control problems and lack of feeling problems aren't my fault or an attribute of the new me. They result from physical problems I have no control over, and they aren't me.

Wow, that's an important and tough realization. Important because it's important to like yourself and be happy with what you do. Tough, because in a way you have to let go of being responsible for your actions. You have to be OK with letting some of yourself go and forgiving yourself.

You have to say "I understand that things are difficult for you, Kevin. Sometimes you act like a total jerk and throw a chair at your wife. But it's not because you're a dick, it's because part of your brain is fucked up. What makes you you has been messed up and makes you not behave like yourself. You aren't responsible for actions like this." That's at least what I've said to myself.

It's really tough but in a strange way, being mad at myself and anger control problems actually make me happy (in a way). When I feel mad, it makes part of me happy because it means that there are still some connections to the feeling part of my brain and the feeling part is still there and working. Sure, it doesn't work real well, but it still works some and it's getting better.

November 24, 1999

393 Days A.A.

Today, I had some interesting thoughts about thinking. I know that people would say I have difficulty concentrating. But I think that the word "concentrating" implies a bit too much. It implies the intensity of the thinking. I think that I can still think with intensity. My problem is that even when I'm concentrating with intensity my

Chapter 24: I'm a Good Person

thoughts go off track. I have trouble controlling what I'm thinking about.

I prefer to call it "compartmentalization." I'm having difficulty separating out my thoughts and keeping them separate. I'm thinking real hard about A and very briefly my thoughts jump to B. Instead of spending a very brief moment rationalizing about what I should be thinking about and going back to my original thought, I wander off and think about B -- just as hard but on B not A. I'm having trouble with compartmentalization in my brain.

That's probably what used to cause my discomfort in large groups of people. Like the time about 10 months ago when my sister took me to a basketball game at the school she teaches at. All the noise was bothering me. I think that my brain was having difficulty deciding what it should concentrate on or pay attention to. It sort of hurt to be in such a noisy, fun environment when there are so many interesting conversations to overhear.

My mind is like a bird with many nests it could rest in. It lands on one nest and then decides can't stay there. It gets up and flies to another nest and the same thing happens again. The bird gets really tired really fast.

I think these anger ~~control~~ misdirection problems are related to my compartmentalization problems. When I get really angry and physically destructive, I'm usually slightly frustrated or upset. When I was "normal" that wouldn't have meant all that much and I would have been able to deal with it pretty well. That was because there used to be a strong barrier between my emotional-feeling part of my brain and the part of my brain that controls my physical actions. But now, things are all mixed up and I have trouble separating the emotional-feeling part of my brain from the physically active part of my brain. Hopefully, I'll build those barriers again.

"Still Rambling Down Life's Road... with a brain injury"

CHAPTER 25
My Sermon

November 25, 1999

394 Days A.A.

At church the other day, Karen and I had to give short sermon-like speeches as a part of a service focused on Thanksgiving. We were supposed to talk about what we're thankful for. Karen spoke before me and informed everyone about what happened to us. Then I spoke. Here is what I said:

My Short Sermon-like Speech For Church

What am I thankful for? Obviously, I have got a lot to be thankful for. I'm standing here in front of you. I have got that to be thankful for. Thankful that I can still stand and thankful that I'm in front of you, not buried somewhere here in Boulder.

As you've heard, I have got a lot to be thankful for. But, the thing I'd like to focus on today is being thankful for being alive. In the next few minutes I'll try to detail my feeling and I'll make a kind of strange comparison.

I was lucky enough to be born in Boulder. I was lucky enough to grow up my whole life in Boulder. Why is that great? Well, for one, the food is great. Now, that's what I'd like to focus on for a bit.

I enjoy the food in Boulder, like all of you do. But it wasn't till a few months after the accident that I really enjoyed the food. I mean *really* enjoyed the food.

Back in December (it was about two months after my accident) was when I first ate food again

Previously, I had sustenance delivered directly into my stomach via a gastrotube button. Later, when I ate again, all food tasted good, *really* good.

It was kind of like what I suppose children must go through, though I don't suppose they remember it. At birth and early in life, their taste buds are more sensitive. As they grow older, everything begins to taste plainer – more everydayish. I suppose if you had every breakfast at Lucile's and every dinner at Q's, I expect they start to taste plain (some days good and some days bad) and more everydayish.

After I started to eat again, it was the same with me. All food tasted really good. Ben and Jerry's and Hagen-Daz ice cream were *really* good. (I would say "It was to die for" but after having stared death in the face for eleven days, I am opposed to saying it that way.) We went to Q's to celebrate our anniversary. It tasted *really* good. Now, I suppose that the taste sensitivity was one of the few good sides of this accident. I'll tell you another.

Like my increased taste sensitivity, I feel the same specialness toward everyone around me. I love the fact that everyone – people I know and people I have never met – is alive. I love the fact that all of you are alive. Take a minute and look at the people around you. When you do that, remember that everyone could be taken away at any instant and everyone is only alive by random chance.

Chapter 25: My Sermon

I feel especially thankful for my wife, Karen, and my son, Andrew.

What I (and hopefully you) have had is a glimpse at how happy we should be that we all are alive. We all should be happy that others are alive – people we are close with and people we don't know.

Everyone contributes so much to this world. We all should be – and I certainly am – thankful. God gave us one *really* important thing that we *all* should be thankful for: existence.

CHAPTER 26
Poorly Aimed Hatred

November 26, 1999

396 Days A.A.

It's interesting, at Mapleton Rehabilitation Hospital I have a chart that goes to all my therapists and they add to it after each therapy session. You'd think that given the thickness of chart, they'd hire a body builder to move it with me, from therapy session to therapy session. I saw a portion of my chart the other day and it says that I have a problem: egocentrism.

What!? I'm egocentric? No way! I discussed it with my therapist for a while and I thought about it some more. She told me I act like I have blinders on either side of my glasses that don't let me see or think about anyone else. At first, I was pissed at the "new me." But then I realized (with my therapist's help) that it's a natural, helpful part of the recovery process.

I'm kind of teetering at the border of it being helpful to only think about myself and of it being helpful to think about others, too. For a while after the accident, I only thought about myself. I remember when it took all of my thought power to swallow the saliva that collects in the back of my throat. Even now, when I'm at work and working during lunchtime, I forget to eat. This happens for two reasons. One, because I think the nerves to my stomach that sense hunger don't work anymore. This is why I've never been hungry since the accident. Two, my mind can only concentrate on one thing at a time. Work and sense hunger? That's too many thoughts at the same time.

So, it's completely natural and good for me to be sort of egocentric. If I lived like this several thousand years ago when getting food was difficult and I wasn't egocentric, I would die from starvation. So, I'm happily egocentric (but then I suppose most people who are egocentric feel that way). I also think it's helpful – that's the difference.

I had an interesting experience yesterday. The day before, I sat at work for five minutes just trying to think of the name of a friend I worked with at IBM. I could picture him and I think he went to grad school with me. But I couldn't think of his name.

But then yesterday, another friend of mine whom I worked with at IBM called and we were talking for a while. He said, "Hey, guess whose wife has a baby."

"Charlie's wife?" I said.

I was right! Charlie is the guy whose name I had been trying so hard to remember the day before and couldn't. When I was talking to my other friend, it popped out easily without me pausing for a second to remember. Talking to my friend from IBM must have helped my memory of the name of another friend at IBM. I think it helps your memory of certain events to be involved with similar events.

When I finished talking him and went into the kitchen with my wife, she was amazed. Not only was I communicating about some science with natural ease, my voice sounded different! The problem I have is called dysarthria (I think) and it makes me slur and sound kind of drunk. It's why we were refused service in a local pub a couple of weeks ago. That caused me to get real mad. I lost control of my anger feelings.

Chapter 26: Poorly Aimed Hatred

I still have dysarthria and I sound different, especially when I leave messages for people on their answering machines. Karen was amazed because when I was talking to my friend from IBM, I sounded like the old Kevin!

It's kind of strange, but I think feelings and memory are closely interrelated. For a long time, I could only remember things that I had a specific incident or action I could attach memory to. Even now, almost always, I need something tangible I can hang my memories on.

For example, only after many times when I sat there and thought about it for a half-an-hour or more, I still can't remember anything about my son, Andrew, when he was young. Oh sure, I remember being there at his birth and what house we lived in when we lived in California. But I can't remember anything else. I can't remember holding him in bed, playing with him at the beach, or what he was like. I have lost all significant memories of him! I hope that much of my memory loss is related to my problem with my emotions and feelings, and when they work well again (and I hope for that, too) my memories of my son when he was real young (birth through three) will come back.

November 28, 1999

398 Days A.A.

Today, I was really pissed off. I was so mad at myself because it was me who caused all that sadness. I did it. I was why my family had to come real fast to the hospital in Minnesota. Dad and his wife Jane had to hop on a plane in England and get an emergency flight back to Minnesota. Why did my whole family converge there? It was because of me. It was me who caused all this sadness.

Today, I felt bad because of all the suffering I had caused. In a way, it was me that caused all that pain. But the physicist in me is used to looking for causes and reasons. Now, I know that some things happen in nature randomly. For example, if an atom is put into an excited state, there is a probability that it will decay within 1 second. There is also a probability (really small) that it stays in the excited state for 100 years. So that's the randomness that applies to quantum systems.

But our cars aren't quantum systems. They are plain old deterministic Newtonian systems that have a reason for every action. Knowing that, I've spent a year searching for the reason for this accident.

This accident happened for a reason. What was it? The only thing I can level on is this: It must have been the fault of that woman who hit us.

Thoughts like that – thoughts of blame – usually piss me off. I get really pissed off, like I did today. The more I try to make sense of the accident, the more pissed off I get.

I would say this is another anger misdirection problem. But in this case, if it is anger misdirection, I think I've chosen a person who deserves it. It's not anger misdirection; it's perfect anger aim.

I think hatred is more than she deserves. Who (except a drunkard) would keep driving so carelessly after two drunk driving arrests? I think hatred draws too much energy from me and is more than she deserves. I think from now on I won't ever think about her. As much as I can, I'll think about just good stuff and as little as I can about her. It's like she never existed.

I recently read this quote from George Bernard Shaw who said, "The worst sin toward our fellow humans is not to hate them, but to be indifferent to them." I guess the sin that the woman who hit us deserves is not hatred, but the worst sin – indifference.

But, today it finally happened! I'm so glad! Ever since my accident happened, I've never cried. Well, that's not exactly true. I have cried. The other day when I was with Mom, I cried a bit. Not cried, whimpered.

Chapter 26: Poorly Aimed Hatred

She was telling me about what everyone was doing when they saw me on my deathbed in Minnesota. She told me about how my brothers, David and Andy, cried a lot. Later, she told me how everyone cried. So, I whimpered . . . for them.

But today I cried for the first time, not for anyone else but for myself! I was crying because I think my life was so screwed up. (Not just my life, but Karen's and Andrew's also.) I have trouble controlling my anger, I think and talk pretty slowly, and probably will never have my job again. And I had nothing to do with the accident. I wasn't driving either car. All this put together made me real sad, and I cried!

So, today I was really sad. I'm so glad that some of this anger has been turned into sadness. That's a big, necessary, and difficult step for me. It means that I'm starting to look at this accident in a new light. This light doesn't focus on blame. It doesn't matter why this accident happened. Any way that it could have happened, it would have screwed up my life.

And my focus shouldn't be on the blame or cause of the accident. That just drags me down and holds my life back to when the accident happened. The accident just happened and I'll never know the cause. Whatever happened happened. Focusing on it will only drag me down.

My focus should be on my recovery and how well it's going. (In a way, it's not *my* recovery. It's my whole family's recovery.) That pulls me up and helps me look forward. Maybe, if I look forward hard enough I can see (from a distance) the bright times ahead. It's thoughts and visions like that this keep me moving forward.

I think a new chapter of my life is beginning. And it promises to be really sad, at least for a while, but just for a while. Maybe past the part of the tunnel I'm under now is a bright place that's filled with happiness.

That's what life is like: a drive through the mountains. You may go through no tunnels but then you've got to round lots of turns and take new directions. But if your life is like mine and has tunnels, it is important that you believe that there will be a light at the end of the tunnel.

I believe there will be light at the end of the tunnel and even in the darkest parts of the tunnel we need to be preparing for the bright happiness that is sure to come.

December 6, 1999

406 days A.A.

The questions of "Why?" and "Why me?" aren't troubling me so much now. There is no "why." It's not just that I can't find the answer. This accident just happened. The important question isn't "Why?" it's "How do I deal with it?" and "What do I do now?"

I think that's what I've been dealing with. I have spent more than a year trying to answer the question "why?" I can't find the answer because there is no answer. I'm ready to tackle the question "What will I do now?"

"Will I teach or help others again?" "How can I help those with similar experiences?" "What can I do to help my family?" These are the important questions now and the questions I should focus my energy on. The "why?" question is so backwards-looking. I should look ahead.

You can't drive through life looking backward at what happened or why it happened as it did. You should drive looking forward at what is to come. That's important because it influences what you're doing now, what direction to move and how you steer.

We're driving down life's road and it's important to steer properly. Steering doesn't control where you've been or even where you are. It controls which direction you're headed. I have to spend my efforts choosing which direction I'm headed and where I'm going. That's what's important.

CHAPTER 27
God, Sugar, and Life

August 21, 2000

465 days A.A.

I just got back from a yearly church camp my church has. It's in a small, rustic collection of buildings near Colorado Springs called La Foret. We had a meeting one afternoon where we filled out a sheet that helped explain who we are. This was helpful for me to write out because it made me consider (and hopefully remember) who I am. Anyway, I still have part of the sheet. Here is what I wrote:

1. Try to remember when you first experienced an awareness of God. Recall the setting, the people present, the particular feeling, and how old you were.

I have no memory of my first awareness of God – that was B.A. I don't remember an exact time A.A., but I have a growing sense of being more present in life and closer to God.

2. Recall the most powerful spiritual moment in your life – times of great feeling, awakening, or decisive events. What happened? What were you feeling? What images of God did they give you?

The accident I experienced was the most powerful moment in my life. A probably semi-sober, terrible driver assaulted us. I have no memory of my feelings then, but I know I feel an intense hatred now.

But, religiously, I am having a growing awareness. The image of God I'm getting is one of sugar.

Sugar is a really complex substance. Not just simple table sugar, but all sugars – those in wheat, milk, meat, and everything we eat. I think that when I took chemistry in high school we had a model of a sugar molecule. The molecule was amazingly complex.

Sugar is complex. That's why we can get so much energy from it. There must be a theorem, or I'll write one if there isn't, that shows that there must be some potential energy locked in complexity. (Is it the second law of thermodynamics?) And the complexity of sugar makes it so useful because it has so much energy locked in it.

Sugar is complex. It is this complexity that makes life possible and propels life forward. We all owe a debt to sugar, for without it life would not be possible. Sugar is not just complexity, but in a way it has good, purposeful complexity.

Plants and bacteria are complex, and plants feed animals. Animals are intimately connected to each other and plants through the chain of life. Animals also have instinct. This instinct compels them to graze or hunt down food (other branches of the chain of life), and procreate (or make the branches of the chain of life longer.)

The pinnacle of the chain of life is humans. (Or so we humans like to think.) Humans have bridged the gap from instinct to purpose. Along with that transition comes the transition from purposelessness complexity to purposeful complexity. A human is much more than a tremendously complex collection of cells. Embedded in the cellular complexity is thought. The complexity of thought is part of the chain of life.

Maybe that's what God is – the vast collection of productive, good, purposeful complexity. Then we humans and our interactions are a small part of God. God is the productive, good, purposed, vast collection of the complexity of the universe.

Chapter 27: God, Sugar, and Life

September 1, 2000

676 days A.A.

I just got back from a canoe trip down the Colorado River. A bunch of us patients at Mapleton went on this four-day trip. Everyone had (or is it has?) a brain injury. I don't remember how everyone got his or hers, though I'm sure I asked. Oh well...

It was a really nice, mellow trip down the river. We started up in the mountains, in a real boxed-in type of place. As we went on the countryside became flatter and more open. On this trip, I got to thinking. (This happens to me on these types of trips, which must be why I like them.) It got me thinking not about what I'll be doing tomorrow, but bigger, more expansive things. This is what I thought:

Life is like a river. A river goes from fast, rushing water being very directed to slower, calmer water in more open places. People have those two traits, too – directedness and openness.

Just like the Colorado River, people often find themselves boxed in with work, family matters, budget, and other business-like stuff. They find themselves working quickly on somewhat mundane but critical matters. They may have check-off list for every day (like I do) of the things they'd like to accomplish for that day. They are goal oriented and their life is fast paced. They are more directed.

Then when you're real directed, often you are more emotionless. At least I am. Emotions don't fit well into job-oriented or task-oriented activities where you're trying to get them done quickly and well. Emotions can't be listed and checked off as accomplishments. As a result, you're more emotionless. Certain things can (or should) open you up and make you more emotional, like deaths or traumatic brain injury.

But at other times, like when you canoe down the Colorado River, you can get a more open, more expansive feeling. You can take time to relax and think about and feel the big things in life. This takes time and that's why it can't happen when you're very directed. You're more open and you feel more things.

When you feel more open, you're more sensitive to others' feelings and your own feelings. You're more emotional. Emotions come from and fit well in a more open life. When you're feeling open and emotional, you can deal with things that really matter, big things that are hard to grasp onto.

And so this is what you do on the Colorado River and in life. When you're more directed, you observe. When you're more open, you feel. Both are needed techniques for assessing something.

I hope that I can be more open. I loved the feeling of going down the river, and I think that's part of what I loved – the feeling of openness. I want to and need to feel that way more. Not that directedness is bad. It's essential and required for success in any activity. But I have to remember that directedness is only half of the equation. I must be more emotional and open.

September 15, 2000

690 days B.A.

I'm still wondering about the questions "Who's responsible for this?" and "What is me?" Obviously, it was almost all because of R----- M----. I think she was about 98% responsible for it. I guess in that case, that would make Karen about 2% responsible for it. Sometimes even that's too much!

But then I probe deeper. Why was R---- such a drunkard? It must have been her friends and the bartenders at the local bar that encouraged her to drink and drive home when she was drunk. But then thoughts like that just get me started.

Who encouraged her friends to drink, and who encouraged the bartender to encourage R---- M----- to drink? For her friends, maybe it was their parents that brought them up with a relaxed attitude

Chapter 27: God, Sugar, and Life

toward alcohol. For the bartenders, it must have been the owner of the bar. But who encouraged the owners? The liquor companies who were pursuing their president's interest must push it on them. The presidents of the liquor companies are only pursuing the interests of the stockholders. In a way, all of society is just a tiny, tiny bit responsible for this accident.

I forgive that woman who hit us.

Maybe when she called us on the night she hit us, she was trying to apologize.

In a way, this woman is not responsible for the accident. What makes her (the drunkard) her? I guess we all have a tiny responsibility. Intellectually, I think I have forgiven the woman that hit us, but only intellectually. I still feel like I could kill her.

October 1, 2000

~~706 days A.A.~~

(I'm ready to stop counting my days like that.)

I'm approaching my two-year accident anniversary. I've been kind of frustrated with the slowness of my recovery. But I've found that if I assume my recovery is over, and that I can't expect anything else to get better, it helps. Then I don't expect anything else to get better, and I'm more thankful for things that come to me. Any recovery I make now I treat as a gift – something I can't expect, and I'm more grateful.

I've been having this picture of my brain and what happened to it. It's rather interesting so I'll write it down in my diary.

My brain used to be like a fried egg – sunny side up. The accident was like an eggbeater and scrambled my eggs. (That's what it did – randomize the complex organizational structure of my brain.) In the end, I have a bunch of beaten eggs that I can simply cook up. Or I can see the things I'm dealing with as good utensils and see this time I have as a good time to start cooking an omelet. I can take a big helping from my cognitive therapist and counselor, add a fair amount of work at CU and love from my family, a dash of Zoloft (my antidepressant) and that's what I am – a gourmet omelet.

I've also been having an image of God rise up in my head. God must be a complex and gigantic collection of all the complexity and beauty in the universe. The reason I'm coming up with this is that I think my continuing recovery from the accident shows me how much we all influence, depend on, and rely on others. I wouldn't be alive if we didn't help each other out so much. In a way, the complexity of the humans is overshadowed by the complexity and interconnectivity of collections of us humans like the emergency response teams and the teams of doctors who saved me.

In fact, much of me is still alive and here because of the cooperation and interconnectivity of the response teams. In essence, part of my existence belongs to them. And I feel that this complexity and interconnectivity is part of God.

My image of God is of a giant sculpture made of clay that continually reforms itself. All of the parts of the giant sculpture are made of the same clay. There are bacteria and plants that are rather simple, yet important, elements of the sculpture. Then there are animals. Animals are also very important parts of the sculpture. But lacking purpose, these are parts that don't really help re-sculpt the sculpture.

Then there are those complex animals called humans that are still part of the chain of life. Their feet are still planted in the soil – the clay – that is made of the plants and animals of the earth. But they're continually forming themselves and each other. They make themselves.

Parents come together and using tiny and simple parts of the clay that are given to them make another part of the sculpture. That must be what is so enjoyable about making love to someone who you're

Chapter 27: God, Sugar, and Life

involved with and cooperate with so much. When you join together physically and emotionally, you must form a small part of God between the two of you.

When you procreate, you pass along a small bit of clay and make a child. Where does a child come from? Part of its structure comes from the vegetables you had for dinner last night. But in the end, the child comes from the earth and the earth's chain of life. That's only the child's raw materials. The organizational structure comes from the parents.

Then a child is born. What do we see in a child that makes us smile? We see possibility. Children are the vast life force of the universe incarnate. We all naturally love babies. Even apes realize that the young need care. Maybe they don't realize why, but they are compelled to take care of their young. There is a life force within them that compels apes to pick up the baby ape and love and care for it. Though they don't realize it, this is because the life force within them is trying to pass itself along.

Children must have in them part of the unbridled life force. That must be why people are intrinsically attracted to them. When they're first born, they're just incredibly complex but small parts of the sculpture. As the child grows, it begins to form itself. As a child grows, its hands are always busy forming its own part of the vast sculpture. Teachers are the well-formed parts of the vast sculpture that help the child form itself. The work of a child is done when the child has grown up. Then that person becomes busy building the vast interconnected networks that humans form.

At our roots, we are all parts of a sculpture. God is the clay. God isn't an individual. Lacking broad enough vision, we have made our vision of God in our own image. But another way of viewing God is as the good, purposeful complexity of the universe, the clay of the self-formed sculpture of life.

"Still Rambling Down Life's Road... with a brain injury"

My image is similar to the image that I remember that Nikos Kazantzakis (author of *Zorba the Greek* and *The Last Temptation of Christ*) wrote about in his *Report to Greco*:

> "Every living thing is a workshop where God, in hiding, processes and transubstantiates clay. This is why trees flower and fruit and animals multiply, why the monkey managed to exceed its destiny and stand upright on its own two feet. Now, for the first time since the world was made, *man has been enabled to enter God's workshop and labor with Him.* The more flesh he transubstantiates into love, valor and freedom, the more he becomes the Son of God."

Being the inquisitive person I am, I still have a bunch of questions (and a few answers that I'm comfortable with, hopefully.)

Aren't we as humans just a collection of cells? Yes. But that doesn't imply or describe well the organizational structure, just as a painting is made of paint, but paint alone doesn't make a picture.

Then, in a way, aren't we all cells in a vast organism? Yes, in part. But the difference is that we have a more complex way to communicate and interact. Cells interact. Marrow makes blood that's used by organs. But our speech, writing, music, and art are more complex methods of communication.

We all are the part of the sculpture. We all are also the sculptors. We help form ourselves. In joining together in cooperative groups, we help make the sculpture grow and become more complex. But what is it that compels us to sculpt?

God is also the life force that drives us onward. Within ourselves we each have a drive to stay alive. I sure it must be within all animals. When I'm squashing ants, they run from me. There was no collective decision and each ant isn't avoiding me out of rational decision making. They all run from me because I threaten their lives and the

Chapter 27: God, Sugar, and Life

life force in them wants to keep on living. Humans have the same life force within themselves.

People's interest in experiencing near death experiences comes from an animal addiction to hormones (endorphins?). People climb high mountains (like I used to), kayak down treacherous rivers, box each other, etc. because they enjoy the feeling of using these endorphins. In essence, they're exercising the life force within them.

I'm not afraid of dying.

Death: been there, done that. I've done that death thing.

I need to find a way that I can ensure permanence. I need to figure out a way to pass along my life essence, to find a way to become a fuller part of God.

All of us have a reservoir of life energy within us. Some people, like firefighters, use it a lot. Others expend their life energy only infrequently. In a sense, they aren't as alive, because when they don't exercise the life force within them, their life force gets rigid.

Not that this is a resounding endorsement for all dangerous sports – some are stupid. But it helps me understand why people are attracted to things like parachuting. This also must be the reason why people are attracted to helping children. People (often mothers, but increasingly so all types) feel a strong need to care for children. It must be that they want to pass along their life force.

The other day in church we read from Hebrews, Chapter 2. It was talking about the relationship of God to Jesus, and Jesus to us. In Chapter 2 it says *"both the one who makes men holy and those who are made holy are of the same family."* Then, if we are Jesus' brothers and sisters, as he called people, isn't God our father? A lot of us Christians profess to know this when we say the Lord's Payer, which starts out *"Our Father,* who art in heaven, hallowed be thy name…" But I don't think that people get this, just as I didn't B.A. This relationship – parent and child – implies that God is a part of us. We are children of God and God is part of us.

But what does all this mean for us? What are we responsible for? (My brain is back again on the responsibility question.) Kids aren't responsible when they're born with Down's syndrome. None of us is responsible that we can't run as fast as Olympic athletes. Our success in school isn't strictly our own responsibility. We may have been born with slow brains, or we weren't trained well when we were young and our brains were growing (up to about age 25 according to the latest studies). If we're not completely responsible for our actions, what are we responsible for?

We're responsible for intent, not ability. We each have to decide on a goal and a course of action. We don't have complete responsibility over whether we can achieve the goal. But our intent is something we control completely. Our intent is entirely something that we decide on and are responsible for.

Some people mean well but are unable. For example, for about a month after I came out of my coma, I couldn't use the bathroom. I wanted to, but I couldn't. (I am assuming so because I can't remember.) Even the more complicated situation of my emotional control problem is an example of this.

I like to take responsibility for my emotions. Don't we all? After all, we like to thing they are what make us what we are. But to what extent am I in charge of them? Most of the time, I completely control my emotional reactions. But then occasionally (but not as occasionally as I'd like) I lash out and get really upset and do stupid things. I did this last week when I stood up at my support group, really pissed off, and beat the door really hard because no one was listening to me talk about how I deal with my thoughts of suicide. I can't control my emotions. In a strange way, I'm not totally responsible for my actions. The problem is that some of the pathways between the feeling part of my brain and the controlling part of the brain are not smooth and are sort of messed up. There

Chapter 27: God, Sugar, and Life

are a lot of signs that say "Construction/Detour" on the pathways in my brain.

Your actions and behaviors that you'd like to think are what make you you are organically based and easily affected or changed. I'm a prime example. We are all more affected by things we have no control over or by random chance than we'd like to think. We all like living, just as I do most of the time. But none of us chooses to be born. We control a lot less that we'd like to think.

The important thing is to realize and help others realize that they're connected to the sculpture, that we all are part of God. Even bad people are part of the sculpture. Saddam Hussein is a part of the body of Christ. Admittedly, he and other evil minded people are really confused cells that are part of the body. They're like a cancer. Cancer is composed of cells of you own body – cells that could be good and important. But they're confused. They don't know what they should do or how they should do it. The problem is they breed fast. So sometimes they need to be excised or put away where they can't do any harm.

The important thing is to remember that we all (even the woman who hit my family) are a part of God. We should try our best and have the strongest intent to work hard and make ourselves a good outgrowth of God. We should pass along God, who is the life force, to others by raising children well, teaching well and doing all that we can do to sustain, preserve and extend life, which is part of God.

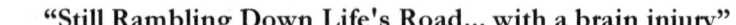 "Still Rambling Down Life's Road... with a brain injury"

CHAPTER 28
What I've Learned Thus Far
(PART III)

"It is this spiritual freedom – which cannot be taken away – that makes life meaningful and purposeful."

—Victor Frankl, ***Man's Search For Meaning***

February 28, 2002

recovery: (ri kuv'ə rē)

1. (< ME recover) The regaining of abilities lost or taken away or restoration or return to health from sickness.

2. (< MF recover) (a) A return to a normal condition. The return toward normal of a particular cell, tissue, or organism after a condition of misfortune. (b) To reapply a material to something. To insulate again or repaint something.

3. (< L to regain, RECUPERATE) To take on again. The getting, or gaining, of something not previously had.

I've recently finished up my first semester teaching back at Carleton College. It went quite well. Granted, initially the administration was unsure of how I'd do. So was I. This last term, I team taught with my department's chair in the classroom. We traded off lecturing.

The term went quite well and next year, I'll be teaching the same course all by myself. In addition, I'll be teaching an upper-level theoretical physics course by myself. That will be a half-time load next year. The year after that, I'll be teaching a full time load then.

I guess that I'm taking on the task of teaching successfully again. I'm recovering. One thing that I've learned in this whole recovery process is that it is essential that you have patience and give yourself time. It will be five years after my injury before I begin to teach full time again. You need to have patience. In addition, you should never expect to return to the same position or expect to do it in the same way. I've been exceedingly lucky.

My severe TBI was easily the most difficult challenge I've had in my life (and it nearly cut my connection to the life force within me). I would never wish it upon anyone. I am still dealing with some of its aftershocks. I think I have used it to improve myself. Granted, something that is extremely critical to my occupation as a professor – my IQ – was quite severely damaged. Yet I think I used the accident and its after affects to improve myself. I am a much more compassionate and sensitive person A.A.. I am also more disinhibited now which has made me more talkative and friendlier. In a way, the accident (or, rather, my response to the accident) has improved me.

Sometimes shit happens. There's nothing we can do about that. We also don't have control over much that we'd like to think we do – like race, overall socioeconomic status, and our intelligence. We all had pretty much the same chance of being born with Down's syndrome. Some of us did, and some didn't. Babies with Down's syndrome did nothing to deserve it and neither did their parents. Sometimes shit just happens.

The one thing that we can control is our attitude and intent. We choose the way to interpret things that happen to us, and we control

Chapter 28: What I've Learned Thus Far...

our intended response. Sometimes we want to do more to help or change situations, but we can't. This could be because we've had a stroke, contracted Alzheimer's disease (as more than 20% of the population that reaches 80 will), or have had a TBI.

However, we always control our intent. Faced with any decision, you can decide what you'll attempt to do. You may not succeed, but you always choose your intent and decide what you'll try to do.

When faced with a difficult situation (which may be self-caused), we shouldn't bang our heads against the problem, but instead we should change our attitude and adapt. We each are like putty balls rolling down the inclined plane of life. The plane is somewhat mottled and rounded, and this causes us to sway along the straight path to the bottom.

But sometimes we may run into a huge cliff that blocks our way. Rather than beat our heads against the cliff time and time again, we need to adapt. We need to become a liquid that molds itself around such immovable obstacles. We can choose to change our expectations and mold ourselves to the immovable obstacles. In doing this, we will find that we often take unexpected turns and sink into unknown loopholes and paths down to the bottom. Like water flowing down an inclined slope, we will find a way to get to the bottom.

The process of adapting to and overcoming these large unchangeable objects that block our progress down the slope of life is challenging and can be very difficult. But overcoming these obstacles can improve us spiritually. In overcoming them, we obtain a well-founded confidence in ourselves and an appreciation of ourselves. Hopefully, we don't take undue credit and our successes bring us closer to the realization of the life force that drives within all of us.

In adapting to unchangeable situations, we can also develop an increased sensitivity to others. We realize that we've only chosen one route around the thing those blocks our path in life and that there are others. We become more appreciative of the routes that others have found. I firmly believe that that is what provides us happiness and satisfaction – bringing happiness to others.

Some of us build the foundations of the houses in which we reside, others haul trash and help keep our environment clean, beautiful and life-giving, still others try to make others happy by serving them an ice-cream cone. We all try to make others happy – even those that spend their day creating weapons of mass destruction and consider using them. In their confused fashion, they are merely trying to bring happiness to their rather limited collection of people they'd consider friends or worthy contributors to society. What they need is not to be put to death (and, in doing so, teach them that the way to solve problems is through murder). We need to protect ourselves and find a way show them the beauty in life and of all others.

I suppose that I've recovered in the last sense of definition two that I quoted above. As a result of my response to the accident, I have gained something I never had before: a sense of God as a process or an impulse that pushes us onward toward the good.

I've thought about it a lot. If God is an all-powerful, good entity, where was God when my accident happened? It couldn't have been some sort of punishment. (If it was, God planned it out very poorly, because I can't see the reason for the pain. And what's the use of punishment if it doesn't clarify injustice?)

God is a process. This means that God was a major part of my recovery. God is the impulse that drives all of us onwards to do good things. Contentment and satisfaction are not godly. As the author Nikos Kazantzakis wrote, God is "the Cry" that drives us onward to more good.

Since the purpose of our existence is to become closer and more helpful to others and to help the community grow and to strengthen God (who is part of the driving force behind the vast collection of the best within us all), this is what makes me and all people happy:

Chapter 28: What I've Learned Thus Far...

Giving to others and helping other people helps us all grow and become more of what it means to be a good human. That is our purpose and hence that is what makes us all happy.

From my memory notebook:

- In every situation, ask myself "What would Jesus do?" before I act.
- Focus on how I am relating to and interacting with people.
- I am still on earth to help and serve others.
- Serve someone each day.

A long time passes...

CHAPTER 29
The Road Goes On

October 27th, 2023

(A quarter of a century A.A.)

What was only a turn of a couple of pages for you was more than two decades for me! I'm very pleased that my recovery from my TBI continues despite (or, perhaps, because of) my response to several challenges that I've had to face. These challenges include the deepest parts of myself -- what makes me the person I am -- and they are my job, my marriage, my understanding of my own life, its purpose, meaning, and my understanding of the Divine process of advancement, which I now name God. I continue to struggle dealing with the changes in my occupation, relationships, and my own understanding of metaphysics. However, at this time, I see considerably more of the environment around me -- I am more "with it" and I am drawing closer to exiting the tunnel that I described previously and which is pictured on the front cover of this book.

The point at which I completed my previous book in 2002, in Chapter 28 of this book, and just after I listed the definitions of the word "recovery" on page 139, I wrote about the professional goals I hoped to achieve which included a continuation of my employment at the Carleton College department of physics. However, in my second year of teaching at Carleton after my accident, my teaching and research skills were evaluated in a way similar to, though perhaps less demanding than, a tenure review. It was decided that I "did not teach up to the standard of Carleton College" and I was dismissed from my position as a professor of physics there.

Accepting this decision was especially difficult for me for several reasons. The main difficulty accepting this was that, like many people, I understand myself largely as a person who works at the occupation that I hold. For me, I was a professor! Now, following this decision of the college, I was told that my teaching was substandard. I was tempted to interpret that to mean that (as a person) I was substandard!

So, in 2003 I returned to my hometown of Boulder, Colorado, and continued to do nanoscale physics research as a volunteer at the National Institute of Standards and Technology (NIST). I put together the thin film deposition system that I designed and for which I had been awarded a grant prior to my TBI from The Research Corporation, an organization in the United States devoted to the advancement of the physical sciences. I had won their Cottrell College Science award in 1998 and was going to receive an acknowledgement of this achievement the morning of the accident which injured me so greatly! However, uncertain that I'd be able to perform the science that I had first proposed in the application, I was forced to reapply for the grant. Some of the ideas I had proposed researching in 1998 had since been discovered and were being researched at two institutions in Germany. So, I proposed other ideas concerning atomic resolution microscopy with the ability to resolve magnetic structure. This grant was also awarded, so when working at NIST in Boulder, I constructed and began creating magnetic multilayers. This was work similar to what I'd been doing in graduate school and my year of postdoctoral research at IBM.

However, I found that I wasn't satisfied working in laboratories because I desired more interaction with others, my colleagues or students: I knew I was capable of doing my nanoscale magnetics

Chapter 29: The Road Goes On

research, but, I didn't like being stuck away in a laboratory. After my accident, I became more of a people person! So, I thought and thought and thought about what I should do with myself…

In a curious way, it was fortunate that a group in the Colorado Division of Human Resources had reviewed my medical situation and determined that I was "permanently and totally disabled" and, being unable to sustain gainful employment, I was able to continue to receive long-term disability insurance benefits, and also Medicare. I suppose that this was, in a way, one "blessing" of my injury and, as a result, I had a substantial amount of time to think about what I wanted to do with the life that was given to me! While I am grateful for the benefits I receive, my lifestyle changed dramatically when living only off of my insurance benefits: I don't own a car or drive myself, I rarely travel, and I live in a "permanently affordable" community that requires all residents to have a pretty low income.

Another "blessing" that came to me because of my injury and my being released from employment in Minnesota was that being a resident of Boulder, which is a reasonably short bus ride from Denver, I came to learn about a theatre company in Denver which featured actors with disabilities. I investigated this group, the Physically Handicapped Actors and Musical Artists League or PHAMALY, and went to see the show "Guys and Dolls" in 2004. It was such a good show and such an effective way for people to see actors, who only happen to live with disabilities, sing and dance in musicals and plays, that I wanted to become part of this effort. Fortunately for me, the next musical produced in 2005 was "Joseph and the Amazing Technicolor Dreamcoat" and I had sung in this musical when I was a graduate student in Illinois ten years earlier! This made it easy for me to learn the music because, though my short-term memory made memorizing new lines and actions difficult, my long-term memory (particularly of music) was still quite robust. So, I joined the cast of Joseph as one of the brothers, knowing the music and only having to remember one line in the show which was one word in length!

This was also true of the next 5 or 6 musicals I performed with the **PHAMALY Theatre Company**: in each of these musicals, I sang a lot but only had one word to deliver as a spoken line. However, as my recovery progressed my memory improved and I was able to take on larger roles like Bert Healy in "Annie", who sings the solo "You're Never Fully Dressed Without a Smile", and Lazer Wolf in "Fiddler on the Roof", who sings the song "To Life" (*L'Chaim*). I was even taken on tour with this company to Tokyo where we performed the musical "Honk" at the Toshima-Ku Art and Culture Theatre in Tokyo! Though I began performing on stage in musicals when I was a child, I'd never played to audiences as large as those in Tokyo -- several *thousand* at each performance!

Though I continue to act with this theatre company, I decided that what I enjoyed about being a professor was my understanding that I was helping others. So I considered deeply how I might make a positive impact on others, particularly those who (like me) society seemed to have dismissed. After sustaining a TBI, and living with various disabilities that I am grateful have diminished in severity significantly since I acquired them, I was surprised at how people at the several churches that I attended in Boulder and Northfield avoided interacting with me after the services, during the social coffee hours. Particularly when my speech was more heavily impaired, people avoided talking with me because it took so much careful attention to understand what I was trying to say. I also feel that sometimes subconsciously people were uncomfortable talking with me when my impairments were so obvious because it required them to face their own vulnerabilities. People were uncomfortable facing the fact that what happened to me could happen to them as they drove home from church!

So, I researched the tendency of religious institutions not accepting and welcoming people living with disabilities (PWD) as members of their congregations as well as the underrepresentation of PWD in communities of faith. I decided that my life's purpose would be to try to help people living with disabilities find houses of

Chapter 29: The Road Goes On

worship of any faith tradition that welcomed them fully. Giving up my goals as a physicist, and donating the thin film deposition system that I designed and built to Carleton College, I began to pursue this new goal of trying to help houses of worship learn to better welcome **all** people. I figured that my experiences as a person living with disabilities would be an asset in this effort, not a professional impediment to be overcome. To do this, I figured that I would need some authorization. So in 2004, I stopped researching at NIST and began to study at the Iliff School of Theology in Denver.

In 2010, I attained a ministry degree -- a Master of Arts in Specialized Ministry (MASM). This took me six years because it was necessary to take three to four buses each way -- a total of six hours of travel each day. Those six hours weren't wasted though because I studied and read for my courses while traveling to and from school.

At the Iliff School of Theology, I studied for an MASM, not a Master of Divinity, which would have allowed me to be an ordained minister. That degree required mastery of Greek or Hebrew, and as I was having such trouble with my memory, I knew that learning an entirely new language was not an option for me. After obtaining my degree, I was granted the honor of becoming a Commissioned Minister in the United Church of Christ. The only disappointment I have from not being appointed as an ordained minister is that, in the UCC denomination, only ordained ministers are called "Reverend". I thought it would be fun to be known as Rev. Kev!

The role of Commissioned Minister is really most appropriate for me because I understand myself as a minister with a particular mission: my ministry is to try and help UCC churches in the Rocky Mountain Conference and nationally to become more welcoming to people living with disabilities. To try and further this goal, I joined the board of the United Church of Christ Disabilities Ministry. In 2012 I was commissioned by this organization, the Metropolitan Denver Association, and my church, the First Congregational

Church of Boulder in a four-way covenant serving as a Disabilities Inclusion Associate.

At that time, I also felt called to expand my efforts beyond the UCC denomination, because there are believers with disabilities of every denomination and religion. For this reason, I began to work with the Jewish Disabilities Advocates, a division of the Jewish Family Services in Denver. They have wonderfully welcomed this disabled Christian minister who tries to assist them in their inclusion efforts. For this I am very thankful, because the work of (and barriers to) inclusion don't really differ among the many religions. In a way, disability, the need to learn to accept it as a fact of life, and the struggles of inclusion efforts, all transcend religious faiths. They are common human struggles!

In addition to my working with the Jewish Disabilities Advocates in Denver, in 2013, I decided to form my own not-for-profit organization that I named **Faith4All** that would be an interfaith not-for-profit dedicated to training faithful organizations to better invite, embrace, include and empower people living with disabilities into active lives of faith in their community. I was fortunate that some people I studied with at Iliff, and others from my church, agreed to form a board and helped this organization obtain not-for-profit status with the IRS.

Although I no longer work as a professor, I still am actively teaching communities how to welcome those people who they may have overlooked. In this way, I am still a teacher and my ministry has become the avenue through which I pursue my mission of helping others. I believe it could be possible that I am doing more good as a minister devoted to helping religious communities learn to welcome everyone, including those people who live with disabling conditions, than I did as a physics professor.

You might wonder why I've listed the various professional efforts that I've undertaken in the last two decades. I've done this to help you (and myself) see the connections between who I was before my

Chapter 29: The Road Goes On

accident and who I am now. I want us to see the similarity that exists between the occupation of physics professor and religious disabilities advocate. I still teach and I still help others. This hasn't changed. In this way, despite the professional challenges that I've faced as a result of my injury, I am still the same sort of person. What has driven me since I was a child -- my curious nature and love of helping others -- drives me still. I invite all those who read these words to contemplate what motivates their efforts in life. *What drives you? How do you hope to change this world for the better?*

My dismissal from my position as a professor of physics and my struggle to reinvent myself professionally, has caused me to carefully consider the role that one's occupation has. Obviously, one reason that people pursue a job is as a source of income. However, I also believe that one's occupation often fulfills a much deeper need: it can serve to define who you are as a person. As an example, my brother David has had a number of occupations in the course of his life: after graduating from high school, he worked in a salmon cannery in Alaska, he was Navy Intelligence Officer for a few years, he became an accomplished carpenter, he received a BA in English in preparation for teaching, and finally entered medical school, received his MD in Emergency Medicine and has, for many years, worked as an ER doctor.

Each of those various occupations helped form the character of my brother David, honing the blade of his personality. He is an active person, who functions very well under extreme pressure. This might explain his attraction to technical rock climbing and kayaking! His ability to maintain focus serves him well when he is working in the emergency room. Everything my brother has chosen to do is an important part of who he is. It is the same way with many of us all. We express ourselves and we come into being by working at our chosen occupation, if we are lucky enough to be able to choose. **We are what we do!**

For the six months I was an inpatient in two hospitals, I considered how I could justify my existence. At first, I decided that my impaired condition was important because people like me needed the life-saving efforts of emergency crews, doctors, and therapists. I thought it was people who were as needy as I was that partly motivated others to act in caregiving ways. I provided jobs!

At the time of these thoughts, I wasn't "firing on all cylinders", and my IQ had been assessed at a pretty low level. But, in my mind, I could see how society benefits from the existence of people in need. I thought it would help make us a kinder, more caring society. But, as time went on, and it became apparent that I would be living with my disabilities for the rest of my life, it was important that I felt that I was providing benefit to society because I was often tempted to think that I was "good for nothing". I had to reinvent myself.

Luckily, most organizations are happy to "employ" people who volunteer. I volunteered as a researcher at NIST and as a tutor in the physics department at the University of Colorado. I joined a community choral group, I joined the PHAMALY Theatre Company, I became more politically active, and I volunteered as a TBI support group organizer. Because I knew I'd never drive again, I earnestly studied and made use of the various modes of public transportation in northern Colorado. In addition to keeping my spirits up, all of these activities provided exercise for my brain and contributed to my recovery.

CHAPTER 30
One Loss

Why do we humans frequently form an intimate loving relationship with another person? Obviously, this drive is built into our nature as animals that propagate sexually. Yet, aside from reproduction, many humans are also drawn to a close relationship because the sharing of burdens can relieve some of life's stresses. It's also fun and satisfying to create a life together with a partner! Personal differences can be helpful to those in a relationship, because the different talents and skills can make the couple more resilient than two isolated individuals. Yet, over time, one partner may decide that the other person isn't contributing to the relationship in ways that are satisfying.

The most important loss in my life was the failure of my marriage to my first love, Karen. I am fairly confident that our marriage would have withstood the common difficulties and challenges of married life. Karen and I had started dating in high school and, though we were apart for four years while in college, we maintained our relationship. After college, we lived together and taught English in Japan for one year. After returning home, we were married in a big ceremony in our home church in Boulder with our families and many friends in attendance. We spent five years studying in Illinois where I completed graduate school. We moved to California for my postdoc where we welcomed our beautiful and energetic baby boy, Andrew. After completing this one year of research at IBM, I was offered a teaching position at Carleton College, my alma mater! Following my first year of teaching, we purchased and moved into a nice home in Northfield. At the end of October of my second year of teaching physics, the devastating accident occurred while we were taking Andrew to daycare before we both went off to work.

The death of our marriage was especially difficult for me because it was through my relationship with Karen that I understood myself. Since we had dated continuously from our junior year in high school, most everyone I was close to knew us as a couple. There was a we that I understood to be more important than I. I believe that Karen felt the same way; however, during the extended time I was in recovery, I believe that she was forced to contemplate her own existence, independent of mine. Even after emerging from a coma, I was terribly impaired and connected with so many tubes. My future condition and ability to provide for a family were in doubt. For many months and even several years, I wasn't in a position where I could contribute meaningfully to the partnership of our marriage.

While our accident and my hospitalization may have marked the beginning of the end of our marriage, I believe it was the personal and professional challenges I faced, combined with the slow pace of my recovery, that caused my wife to lose hope in the recovery of our relationship. The repair of the brain can be frustratingly slow! If you break your arm, your bones will set and regrow structural integrity within months, and the progress of healing is almost always unidirectional. This is not true of repairs to a damaged brain. Reconnecting and regrowing new neural pathways takes time!

Although a large amount of healing after a traumatic brain injury takes place within the first three years, significant recovery can proceed for many years, even decades. This was certainly the case with me. Even casual acquaintances (e.g. the administrative assistant of my investment broker) continued to notice and inform me of

Chapter 30: One Loss

significant improvements in the clarity of my speech as late as a decade after my injury! Such slow recovery can be difficult to detect for people who are with you frequently, but noticeable to casual acquaintances infrequently seen.

In addition, this slow pace is not always unidirectional. Sometimes a person recovering from a TBI can slide backward in their recovery and old problems or behaviors can rear their ugly heads after they're thought to be overcome. Deterioration following an initial recovery of abilities has been seen, particularly in older survivors, but isn't necessarily a given. I believe that it is helpful for those recovering from their TBI to remember to keep their minds active, and always keep learning! Mental workouts keep your brain active and facilitate the growth and complexity of new neural connections. This never has to end! Though significant neural growth is very common for some years following a TBI, keeping your brain actively engaged with reading or listening to books, staying physically fit, meeting new people in support groups or in community organizations can extend one's recovery for many more years.

While I found that I had no other option than to recover slowly from my injury, my wife wasn't able to live with this situation. She wasn't able to live with my challenges and impairments, just hoping to see the return of her old Kevin. After trying to live with and love the "new" person that I was, Karen decided that she would be happier beginning a new life without the burden of an unknown recovery outcome for me. After several sessions of "marriage counseling" (which felt more like "divorce preparation"), we divorced in 2001.

A few years after our divorce, my ex-wife began dating and eventually re-married. While I have had a few intimate relationships following our divorce; they haven't worked out and I am single again. I wonder if this will remain the case forever. I am unsure of this and have become philosophical concerning the issue of romance, love, and relationships.

Looking back on the ending of our marriage, I am pleased with how we decided to co-parent our son. For the first few years following our divorce, we weren't especially friendly to each other, though we never fought or battled over custody of our son. This is an agreement that we came to as our marriage was dissolving: we would always maintain a friendship for our son's sake. We both agreed that it was important that he be raised by both of us and that we would be at least civil to each other, if not friendlier. Our work as co-parents resulted in a healthy and happy son. Andrew graduated from Tufts University and now studies at Dartmouth Medical School. He is engaged to Andrea, a fellow medical student. They want to work in emergency medicine somewhere in the West.

Thinking about intimacy and close relationships from a more philosophical angle following my near-death experiences and significant recovery from such an impaired state has led me to consider more generally the nature of human life and human relationships. Today, sitting here recording my thoughts on a computer, I am obviously an individual who is alive. However, I wonder to what extent I am alive, and to what extent I am an individual. Let me deal with these two seemingly simple questions separately.

What is it to be alive and how is life manifested or enacted? Simply the existence of your body, a collection of a large number of cells, is not sufficient proof of life. For many days following my injury my body existed, though I was only kept alive by artificial means -- heartbeat monitors and regulators, artificial ventilators, feeding tubes, and a shunt relieving the pressure on my brain. I was in a deep coma. My doctors had been looking for my brain's response to external stimuli but measured none. Slowly, like layers of onion skin being peeled away, my eyelids opened and eventually my eyes sometimes tracked activity outside my body; however, this was not proof of response.

Chapter 30: One Loss

On the eleventh day of my coma, the neurosurgeons called a conference where my family was informed that I would probably never be fully cognisant and would need to live in a care facility for the rest of my life. They suggested withdrawal of life support, saying "Some things are worse than death." They said purposeful response is a key measure of cognition. Though my mom remembers my clenching her hands occasionally as she talked to me, the doctors told her that this could be simply involuntary contractions of my muscles. My family knew that I needed to demonstrate purposeful response to commands in order to show that I was "there" and capable of learning skills.

My mom and sister left the family conference and came to my bedside in the neuro-ICU. My sister said, "Kevin, raise your arm." There was no response from me. Again, she said, "Kevin, you have to raise your arm." And then, from somewhere deep inside a terribly damaged brain, came commands to my arm; my arm lifted high. I was "there", responsive, and able to follow commands!

To anyone who knows my story, it is obvious that I am alive and doing so well because of many people: the emergency crews at the scene of my accident, countless doctors, nurses, and therapists, and my family, for believing in me and supporting my determination to recover as fully as possible. Yet, not only I rely on others to live. This is true of everyone!

Essentially, we humans exist as independently as do the various cells in a tree: each one is different and performs a different function for the tree to stay alive. However, cells are not really independent. They work together. Each cell in a tree relies on other types of cells for nourishment. On a tree, the bark can't really live without the leaves, and the leaves require a trunk and roots for their survival. This is true of humans, as well. Though different, we each rely on a community of others to live well.

The important thing for us to do is to live our lives with this awareness. This is one of the valuable lessons that I've learned because of my injury and recovery. Undoubtedly, I wish that I was able to learn this in an easier way! But my knowledge of the connectedness of all life is more than simply an intellectual concept: I feel that this understanding is in every fiber of my body and it is always deeply seated in my thoughts. For that, I am very thankful!

CHAPTER 31
Metaphysics and Life's Purpose

Looking back on my experiences recounted in this book, I can see the growth of a significantly injured man-child (who used diapers for some time at the age of 31!) and the many challenges he faced (some of which he has overcome). I can see a person who struggled to recover, a person working to make himself into a person he values, be that a physics professor and a husband, or a minister, family member, and friend. In this book, I read of someone as he was changing.

Although the changes to my life and personality resultant from my TBI might have occurred more quickly and in a more obvious way than for others, *do not we all continually change when living life?* Being alive is all about change, be it the purposeful response I evidenced when resting in a coma, or the efforts I now make to assist faith communities at improving their response to people living with disabilities in their congregations. Indeed, change is the only true constant in the universe!

As sentient beings with choices of how we respond to changes in our environment (and selves), we have the opportunity to take a path toward a greater life -- one filled with more peacefulness, vitality, diversity, and justice -- or we can choose to follow the push of the second law of thermodynamics toward greater randomness and the destruction of complexity. This path leads towards self-centeredness, conflict, warfare, and death of both people and productive ideas that can guide us. Which path we follow is a choice made constantly.

I don't have a philosophical understanding of what drives the increase in complexity, I only observe it all around me in almost all systems. Granted, the destruction of complexity is inevitable -- be it represented by a beautiful sandcastle on a beach washed away as the tide rises, or the intricate and delicate physical structures sustaining a human life which disintegrate upon death. The continual drive toward the destruction of every isolated system, the increase in entropy (or randomness of physical objects) is a manifestation of the second law of thermodynamics, which **always** occurs in **every** isolated system.

The only violation of this process toward unstructured randomness occurs in open systems, systems that are not isolated and interact (or exchange energy) with something outside the system. (Making a very considerable jump in size and complexity, I believe that this second law of thermodynamics also applies to human societies: those societies that are insular and reject influences from other cultures, are destined not to advance as rapidly in a way beneficial to all people. But, I digress…)

However, we all can see from the evolution of life on earth, the growth and learning of us all as individuals, and the increase in the complexity of our human societies, that there exists a drive in the open systems in which we live toward increased complexity. Be it the formation from inert molecules into single-celled organisms, or the grouping of humans into clans, cities, or states, all things in existence are a result of a process of increasing complexity and diversity.

The importance of valuing diversity shouldn't be underestimated because it is due to diversity that we attain strength. This fact was highlighted in the science fiction of the many and diverse *Star Trek* productions. For example, the crew of the starship Enterprise was made stronger and adapted more easily because of the cultural diversity of her crew. Humans, from a variety of cultures, Vulcans, and even Klingons were needed to effectuate the mission to seek out

Chapter 31: Metaphysics and Life's Purpose

new life and new civilizations and to boldly go where no **one** has gone before! (This fictional TV series is little more than an allegorical representation of the multicultural society of the United States, its strengths as well as its weaknesses.)

What drives, gives impulse, or lure along the path toward increasing complexity? This is a question that I've considered for about 25 years, but remains unanswered in my mind. My studies of this question have led me to a philosophical understanding called **process philosophy**, of which I was unaware prior to my injuries. Though scholars can see precursors to or elements of process philosophy embedded in the work of earlier philosophies, the mathematician/scientist who became a philosopher named Alfred North Whitehead wrote the revolutionary book **Process and Realty** in 1929 which introduced a novel metaphysics that sees the importance of events, or interactions, as more fundamental to reality than the bits of matter distributed in space. It is an entirely different way of understanding the fundamental elements in the universe.

One can find the earliest seed of this "ontology of becoming" in the writings of Plato, who attributed to Heraclitus the quotations "everything changes and nothing remains still", and "you cannot step twice into the same stream". Process philosophy, or as Whitehead named it "philosophy of organism", posits that all reality is comprised of interacting events, which are more fundamental and measurable than the mere existence of matter. I believe it likely that part of his motivation when conceiving of this notion came from quantum theory which also was being developed at this time. In quantum mechanics (of which I am very familiar), and also in process philosophy (of which I am not an expert), the position of a very small object (like an electron) when traveling in space can never be known exactly. In fact, as the oft repeated double-slit experiment demonstrates, an electron doesn't have an exact position until it is measured! It is the event of the measurement of the position of the electron that determines its location. According to Whitehead's philosophy of organism, we humans are each, as individuals, a "society of events", over which only a very small portion do we have any control!

Process philosophy has had a significant impact on the more general study of philosophy in the 20th and 21st centuries. Other philosophers, like Charles Hartshorne, David Ray Griffin, Arthur Peacocke, and John B. Cobb, have further expanded on the ideas of process and becoming, particularly on the process-understandings of God. In addition, this philosophical movement has had a significant influence on fields of study other than philosophy and religion: there are movements within the fields of mathematics, biology, ecology, medicine and psychology that resonate strongly with this philosophy of organism.

For this reason, it is the interaction with other actual entities that life is shown to exist. Just as I was first judged to be cognisant when I raised my arm in response to my sister's pleading, the existence of anything is shown through its interaction with other objects or actual entities. Following my severe injuries, at first the cells in my body were simply being pushed and prodded by external machines which kept me alive, working against the second law of thermodynamics. Though sustained in a coma by external medical means, I don't know if you could say that I was truly alive, because life interacts with the surrounding environment and causes change or advancement to occur.

However, raising my arm in response to my sister's pleading demonstrated that I had cognition! For a while, my life was sustained by the external means of mechanical ventilators and a gastrostomy tube ("G-tube") which fed me. I'm sure that I had many other connections to various devices attached to my body, the scars of which I can still see on my arms and torso. As my recovery progressed, these important, life sustaining attachments were withdrawn. After about four months, I began to speak by saying more than "yes" or "no" in response to questions posed to me. So as my recovery continued, although my need for and interactions

Chapter 31: Metaphysics and Life's Purpose

with external means of life support decreased, my ability to interact with my environment increased. I was becoming more fully alive!

Shortly after my dismissal from inpatient stay at Craig Rehabilitation Hospital I began to teach again, first as a teaching assistant and then as a professor. I followed this path because, despite my memory impairments, this was the life that I knew and expected. Just before moving back to Carleton College three years after my injury, I was discussing the nature of God with a Religious Studies professor. I told him that I didn't believe in God because I couldn't understand how a God could have allowed or caused my accident to occur. I told him that I know that I wasn't always a good person when growing up and hurt others; but I could see no justification for what had occurred to me. Additionally, I survived my injuries and much worse things happen to other people every single day!

He asked me, "Why do you continue to attend our church if you don't believe in God?" I responded by telling him that what we discussed in church -- focusing on living a productive life, caring for others, and all humanity's oneness in God -- this helped me to become a better person, to change from a self-centeredness induced by my trauma to an individual caring for the welfare of others. He said something like "Oh, you're talking about Process Theology!" It was the direction pointed to by this professor which sparked my interest in Process Theology and Process Philosophy.

My studies of Process Philosophy and Theology have provided me with an understanding of the nature of reality and religious belief with which I am comfortable. It is with this understanding of the process of becoming, of the philosophy of organism, that I understand my recovery from such an injured state. It informs my view of the world today. Within me is the drive for enlivenment, which is a natural result in this universe becoming.

The inevitable lure to the greater, the becoming of the universe which counteracts the drive toward randomness, is embedded in the nature of reality. This can be understood as the natural result of the fact that mere destruction is itself a self-defeating process which leads to an empty set universe. I mean, if you break things up and destroy the complex interactions of their parts, you will end with a bunch of useless crap! The results of the second law of thermodynamics predict randomness, structurelessness, the death of all things. However, creativity and creation (which is all around us) is the only process that can lead to something greater, something more than randomness. This drive of creativity follows the French philosopher Heri Bergon's lure (*èlan vita*l) or "the call" described by one of his students, Nikos Kazantzakis, the author of "Zorba the Greek" and one of my favorite authors!

Being of limited understanding and lifespan, unable to easily conceptualize this process of becoming, and not able to perceive its action underneath all changes in the world, many people throughout all history, personalize (or humanize) this process and call the result "God". Largely, we humans have formed our understanding of the process that drives the enlivenment of our world as being the results of a controlling entity called "God". Being somewhat limited in our ability to conceptualize the unseen, we *humanize* the process of enlivenment, making it into a powerful entity to which we pray for forgiveness and assistance in our efforts.

Thus, this process of humanization results in a diversity of different conceptions of God, which are culturally specific responses to basic human needs and challenges suggested by this question: *How can one best live a life that promotes an enjoyable, peaceful, and productive society?*

This doesn't limit or restrict the importance of the concept; but it does allow for a diversity of equally valid understandings that promote the health of the earth's community. This process-based understanding of God does not imply that I am not a Christian. Just as I cannot live today uninformed by my past, my understanding of Christianity is that it promotes the well-being of all life and doesn't

Chapter 31: Metaphysics and Life's Purpose

limit or deny other understandings God. Obviously, others who call themselves Christian don't agree with me. But I maintain that I am a Christian. Having lived in Japan for one year and having studied Zen Buddhism there and over the course of the last few decades in the United States, I see and experience the benefit of Zen meditation, the almost daily practice I have found especially helpful. As I see it, there is very little functional difference between Zen meditation and Christian centering prayer, an activity in which I have participated formally, and have been featured in a video and online course by Father Thomas Keating titled "Centering Prayer".

My understanding of Christianity is **not** the same understanding as many people who call themselves Christian! Yet, my functionalist understanding of reality and religion works for me and guides me to act in a way more beneficial to others and to my environment. To the extent that their religious beliefs guide them similarly, I see no problem with others' understanding, even if they differ from mine. Nothing more should be expected of anyone! The importance of belief is not so much in its truth or falsity as determined by an observer, but how such beliefs change or influence the actions of those holding such beliefs.

In this way, my experience with the severe and consequential injury recounted in this book has led me to a more placid understanding of myself and the world. My experiences recovering from a severe Traumatic Brain Injury have always been a struggle -- a struggle to breath, to walk, to think, and to remember. And the struggle continues on: I struggle to operate my not-for-profit **Faith4All**, I struggle to memorize lines and act more expertly in productions of the **PHAMALY Theatre Company**, I struggle to sing more lyrically. I also work to be a good father to my son. I make an effort to be a good son, brother, and cousin. Yet, continually, as I make these efforts, I rest confident that I make these struggles in response to the Divine Lure, *the call* that I perceive.

This Divine Lure can be understood as the voice of God, the drive toward greater complexity and vitality, or the *èlan vital*. It does not matter. What matters is that we all, in our various and different ways, stride forward on this path toward greater complexity, vitality, and peacefulness. I hope that reading this book, learning of the common effects of TBI, and seeing these consequences as magnified but similar to the struggles that we all face, will help you navigate this journey you're all on as well!

APPENDIX
For Survivors

I've included here an annotated list of sources of information that may be helpful for those with a TBI, those close to one with a TBI as well as acquaintances. The list is by no means complete or without personal bias. It's simply a list of those things that I found useful.

For a person with a TBI:

Over My Head by Claudia L. Osborn (Andrews McMeel, 1998)

This book is written by a medical doctor who suffered a TBI. She has worked hard a come back to become a practicing doctor again. On her website homepage she writes: "I am a survivor of traumatic brain injury. I am also a doctor (a Ph.D.-type) who has written a book about my experience and my successful rehabilitation. My purpose was to explain what living with a brain injury means to the survivor, to the 'significant other' and family, to the rehabilitation professional, and to communicate the knowledge that it is possible to create a fulfilling new life and move beyond grieving about what has been lost."

Halfway Home: My Life 'til Now by Ronan Tynan (Scribner Publishers, 2002)

This is the autobiography of the famous Irish tenor who was born with problems in his legs and had them amputated below the knee when he was 20 years old. It is quite an amazing story to read. This fellow has incredible drive! He is a world class singer, an athlete and a doctor! Please don't feel that you should have the same motivation, but it is good to have good examples of how you can overcome terrible obstacles in life.

Man's Search for Meaning by Victor E. Frankl (Washington Square Press, 1959)

Victor Frankl was committed in a concentration camp in World War II. Inside, he questioned the reasons behind and meaning of existence. I was struck with the same sorts of questions and had difficulty finding a reason to live for quite some time.

www.brainbook.com

The BRAIN BOOK® System is a complete, home-based cognitive retraining program for persons with brain injury (TBI and ABI) who wish to acquire compensatory skills for the purpose of maximizing cognitive function. They have a very useful website that I've listed above. The program has been successful for people with mild, moderate and severe injuries.

The BRAIN BOOK® System is appropriate for people with brain injury who: are able to read and write (minimum of grade 3 level), possess self-awareness/insight (or are capable of acquiring it), are highly motivated to function at their maximum vocational potential, and are willing to independently commit the necessary time and energy to complete the program successfully.

APPENDIX
For Supporters

<u>**For a loved one, family member, friend, or acquaintance of someone with a TBI**</u>:

A Grief Observed by C.S. Lewis (Bantam Books, 1961)

      C.S. Lewis is probably one of the greatest Christian writers of all time. I found this book very helpful and think that it would be helpful for a family member of a TBI survivor coping with and coming to terms with having a relationship with someone with a TBI.

Confronting Traumatic Brain Injury by William J. Winslade (Yale University Press, 1998)

The Diving Bell and the Butterfly by Jean-Dominique Bauby (Vintage International, 1997)

      Talk about interesting! Mr. Bauby sustained a TBI when he had a stroke that left him unable to control any muscles in his body except his eyelids. Then, after working out a communication system with nurses and therapists, he was able to "write" the entire story by blinking his eyelids. I found the book very inspiring and it guided me and helped me see how much life the brain alone can live.

Coping With Mild Traumatic Brain Injury by Dr. Diane Roberts Stoler (Avery Publishing Group, 1997)

Dr. Diane Roberts Stoler, Ed.D., a health psychologist and professional speaker, sustained a stroke from a cerebral bleed and two traumatic brain injuries (an auto accident and brain surgery). Her book, *Coping With Mild Traumatic Brain Injury*, describes the most common physical, mental, and psychological symptoms of brain injury, explaining why each occurs and what can be done about it, as well as offering practical suggestions for coping with the problem.

Memento and Following by Christopher Nolan

(Faber and Faber, 2001)

This an interesting book and the movie *Memento* especially excellent. It does an extremely good job of giving the viewer the feeling that accompanies anterograde amnesia, the short-term memory troubles that are extremely common to a TBI.

Understanding Brain Injury: Guides from the Mayo Clinic

These are a set of guides that are produced by the Mayo Clinic in Rochester, MN. The Mayo Clinic has run a study of recovering from a TBI and has set up a "Traumatic Brain Injury Model System Center". They are a good contact and have a website at www.mayo.edu/model-system/index.html that is very useful. Some information is contained in some guides that the center has written that are available by downloading the Adobe PDF files. The links are: Understanding Brain Injury: A Guide for the Family and Understanding Brain Injury: A Guide for Employers which are both accessed through www.mayo.edu.

VISION

I am water flowing down a river. I always flow.
As a rough stream, a small creek, then a river
I came down the mountains.
As a deep river, I should have continued on.

But then, I was struck.
Winter's cold – unending unconsciousness – froze my motion.
But I am water and would not stop long.

Like the Niagara plummeting over its falls, my path changed.
Arriving at the foot of the fall, at first I was rough.
I was a child again flowing down the mountains.
But I am water and I flow on.

Where will I go? I do not know.
But the constant flow has revealed this:
Water's flow will not stop.
    Cold may freeze its surface,
    Rocks may get in its way,
    Humans may divert it,
    But water will flow.

And through it all, vision helped me navigate the river.
This vision is not a picture of what should be,
It is the ability to see the landscape change as the river runs on.
With vision, I celebrate the continuous flow of the waters of life.

By Kevin Pettit

Printed in the USA
CPSIA information can be obtained
at www.ICGtesting.com
LVHW040331030624
781956LV00002B/16